EXPERIENTIALISM

INTEGRATING MIND & BODY, SPIRIT & MATTER, THE MANY & THE ONE

G. MICHAEL BLAHNIK

IA&A Books
Cincinnati, OH, USA
Copyright: 2011 by G. Michael Blahnik
All rights reserved.
ISBN: 13: 978-1460928356
ISBN: 10: 1460928350

Library of Congress Control Number: 2011904146

Visit www.CreateSpace.com to order additional copies.

EXPERIENTIALISM

INTEGRATING MIND & BODY, SPIRIT & MATTER, THE MANY & THE ONE

Contents

PART 1: A Brief History of "isms" and "ologies"

1. The Problem of the One and the Many

Philosophy, if not all of human life, can, I think, ultimately be understood within the context of the one versus the many. Is there one, absolute, objective reality from which we human beings draw our various and often conflicting perspectives? Or are there as many realities as there are people, realities in which all people are correct and from which no person can escape? Plato advanced the absolutist, objectivist thesis that there is only one reality, the reality of forms. The forms are ultimate, perfect, and unchanging realities, whereas earthly realities are but mere shadows of the forms. The shadows are not true realities, but they might participate from time to time in the true realities of the forms (Plato, 1986). Plato's contemporary, Protagoras, advanced a relativist, subjectivist thesis that maintained that everyone has his or her own reality and that all of these realities, even if they conflict with each other, are right (Plato, 1992).

Objectivism appeals to all people inasmuch as all people know that there are at least some aspects of the world they inhabit that are what they are, regardless of how people might understand them to be. Relativism also appeals to all people inasmuch as all people know that there are at least some aspects of their own experience that cannot be verified directly by other people but are, nevertheless, real to those individuals who experience them. It seems that these two opposing reality assumptions are inescapable aspects of that which we call reality. It just depends upon the individuals involved as to *what* they consider to be objective and *what* they consider to be relative.

It seems also that the closer we get to *who we are*, the more objectivist we tend to be. And the further away from *who we are*, the more relativist we tend to be. If an evolutionist and a creationist discuss the aesthetic qualities of a work of art, they might very well advance two opposing opinions about the work, while neither of them would care to come to blows over their differences. But when they get on the topic of evolution and creation, they might very well get heated and aggressive during their discussion. Now, if an aesthetician gets into a discussion with a logician, where the aesthetician advances the reality of beauty in ambiguity and the logician advances the un-reality of contradiction, these two people might very well get heated and aggressive in relation to each other. Whereas, if these same two people advanced their opinions about evolution and creation, neither of them might ever think of touching the other in an aggressive manner or of raising his or her voice in dispute. It seems to matter very much to us *who we are*, regardless of *what we believe*.

The evolutionist is in good part defined by his (let's say) adherence to the theory of evolution. And the theory of evolution accounts for reality (of which he and everybody else is a part) by claiming that reality is reducible to changing patterns of energy (sub-atomic particles) through time. Whereas the creationist is in good part defined by her (let's say) adherence to the theory of creation. And the theory of creation accounts for reality (of which she and everybody else is a part) by claiming that reality is something created and sustained by God.

Both evolutionist and creationist are advancing a traditional objective claim. The claim seems to rest upon that objectivism in all of us that makes us who we are. When *who we are* gets challenged or threatened, we tend to respond with our whole being, physically and mentally, or physically, mentally, and spiritually. It is the objective aspects of us that we identify with. When these aspects are challenged or threatened, *we* are challenged or threatened. And when we are threatened, we tend to defend ourselves, often times aggressively.

Protagoras might argue that both evolutionist and creationist are right: the evolutionist is right for him and the creationist is right for her, and since neither of them can get outside of their own understanding of reality, then both understandings must be right. The creationist might convince the evolutionist of the validity of her own ontology and, simultaneously, the invalidity of his ontology, and hence gain a convert. But this does not mean that the creationist has somehow pierced the bubble that constitutes her ontology and entered into the realm of objective reality. Rather, it means that she has managed to convince the evolutionist of the error of his ways. But was the evolutionist in error? How could the evolutionist be in error if every person's reality is right?

2. Realism: The Original Objectivism

The term "realism" has been applied to many areas of human life, and each of these areas has its own slant on what this term means. I wish to define realism in a particular way, even though this way might differ slightly from the traditional ways the term is used in philosophy and other areas of human endeavor.

Simply put, realism is an ontology (reality structure) that asserts that there is one world apart from the human mind, whether that world consists of material and/or immaterial beings, and that this world, or at least aspects of it, can be directly known to us as it is and not simply as we understand it to be. Understood in this way, realistic ontologies comprise the bulk of western philosophies, religions, and world views prior to Descartes and the modern Western era. Animistic ontologies, where the world around us is comprised of spiritual entities with natures of their own, Platonic forms, where the world around us is but a shadow of the real world of forms, and the theistic ontologies, where a powerful immaterial spirit creates less powerful spirits as well as de-spirited beings (material objects) are all examples of realism.

But ancient and medieval realism were dominated by supernatural beings. These beings usually had power over people and nature. Throughout this work, supernaturalism will be viewed as an original form of rationalism, but its rationalistic foundations were not experienced as rational, i.e. as mental. Rather, they were experienced as realistic. God and things supernatural were believed to exist as realistic, objective beings. Hence, I will include supernatural ontologies under realism. But it should be kept in mind that underneath this realism lay a deeper rationalism. Supernaturalism will be understood ultimately as a world of the mind or mental phenomena writ large, or reified. After Descartes and the development of science, supernaturalism was returned to its origin by collapsing into the mind. I hope that this way of understanding our ontological past will become clearer as this work unfolds.

3. Theistic Realism: Reified Rationalism

Theistic realism asserts that God is an objective immaterial being who would exist as he is whether human beings existed or not. According to theistic realism, this knowledge of God is not conjured up by our own minds. It is either 'implanted' in us by God himself or 'communicated' to us by God, nature, and/or some other beings or forces. We might not be able to grasp or understand the fullness of God, but that does not detract from the 'fact' that God is the ultimate source of our objective knowledge of him. Without God there would be no human mind to have knowledge of him or anything else.

Aquinas argues that God is an intelligible light that has created a lesser light of intelligence (people), but this does not mean that the human light of intelligence must understand God as a being entirely conditioned by the limitations of human intelligence. To do such would be to align with relativism. Rather, the reverse is the case for Aquinas. That is, human beings can grasp the essence of God because the greater intelligence (God) has the power to overcome the limitations of the lesser intelligences (people). "Therefore it is not necessary that every creature should require a superadded light in order to see the essence of God," (Aquinas, 1960). Aquinas argues that the created light of human intelligence is a necessary but not sufficient condition for a human being to grasp the essence of God. We need our intelligence to be awakened by the intelligence of God, but we cannot wrap our intelligence around God. Rather, as it is written in Psalms 35, 10: "*In Thy light we shall see light.*" It is the light of God that is objective and unchanging reality. It stirs human intelligence and allows us to see it as it is, i.e. its essence, even though we are not capable of understanding all aspects of God.

Theistic realism has also asserted that human beings are made of body and soul and that the soul can be divided into parts. Augustine writes that "there are three kinds of vision" [soul functions]: corporeal, spiritual, and intellectual. The corporeal vision is that of our senses; the spiritual is "whatever is not of a body, and yet is something" i.e. signs of things formed in the mind (e.g. a thought or image of a bodily thing), and the mental is our understanding of the signs of things formed in the mind (Augustine, 1964). Augustine uses the sentence "Thou shalt love thy neighbor as thyself" to exemplify. He says that we can see the letters on the paper by virtue of our sensual soul; we can form an image of our neighbor in our minds by virtue of our spiritual soul; and we can understand the meaning of love and the other words we use by virtue of our intellectual or mental soul.

But all of these visions are manifestations of one soul, i.e. an unextended, incorporeal being that rules over the body, which is corporeal and extended in space. Our soul 'sees' through the senses, the imagination, and the understanding. Sensual knowledge is the least important, imaginative knowledge next, and understanding (imageless things) the most important form of knowledge attainable by the soul.

The soul, for Augustine, is real and objective. It has a nature of its own, regardless of what anyone might think or claim. It does not depend upon or derive from the mind of a person. Rather, the mind of a person is an integral part of the soul. Also, the soul could exist without the body, but the body could not exist without the soul. But if the soul exists without a body, then that soul is not human, for a human must be necessarily composed of body and soul (Augustine, 1964). Hence, though soul is greater and more self-subsistent than the body, the body is a necessary aspect of the human soul. It is just not a necessary aspect of God, i.e. the supreme, body-less soul.

Contemporary Christian understanding of the mind:body problem that so bothers science and modern thinkers organizes reality into three substances: spirit, mind and matter. These substances are arranged hierarchically, with spirit on top and in control of the other substances. Spirit (Augustine's intelligence or understanding) in its eternal and unchanging form (God) created and sustains everything other than itself. It (God) created and sustains the spirit, mind, and body of all human beings. The human spirit (Augustine's intellect or understanding) is that which understands God's existence and wills the mind and body to act; the mind (Augustine's spirit) is that which understands the physical world around itself and operates in conjunction with that world. It is that which thinks, cogitates, calculates, reasons, etc. The body is the matter that is acted upon by the mind and the spirit. The mind acts upon the body (and other physical bodies outside of the mind) by understanding and manipulating them in accordance with our understanding of them. (This is what science generally does.) The spirit acts upon both mind and body by understanding the mind and body to be creations of the eternal and unchanging spirit (God) and by willing the mind and body to act in particular ways. (This is what science generally denies.)

In Christianity spirit has an existence of its own. It exists whether or not there are other spirits or minds to understand it. It is the reason other spirits and minds exist. This spirit imparts itself to other spirits (human beings) and sustains their existence. The spirit of human beings can understand the essence of God because it 1) shares God's nature and 2) can be overcome by the power of God. Animals, though created by God, cannot understand God's essence because they 1) don't share His nature (do not possess spirit) and 2) don't possess a mind that admits of recognizing God's power.

In Christianity mind has an existence that is both realistic and dependent. The mind exists on its own in that it has control over the body, but its existence is dependant upon the spirit, ultimately the spirit which is God, and not upon the body, which is generally the claim of science. The mind is an active agent in relation to the body and the bodies of nature. It acts upon the body through understanding it and willing it to perform actions. Here, modern Christianity's 'mind' is similar to medieval Christianity's 'understanding' or 'intellect'. Science, it seems, has challenged the existence of God and the spirit he has supposedly imparted to human beings by replacing God with matter or energy and inverting the dependent relationship between mind and body. Such a challenge has altered Christianity's understanding of the mind. It has elevated the mind to the status of something capable of understanding abstract ideas (including the idea of God) in addition to understanding the body and the bodies of nature. In the modern world of science, the existence of a human spirit or a divine connection is virtually gone.

Psychology has reframed the existence of the soul into the existence of the self, divesting the soul of much or all of its supernatural force. Modern Christianity is much more amenable to the idea of a three part system of human nature comprised of: self – mind – body, where self dominates the mind and the mind dominates the body. Understanding reality in these terms allows Christianity to keep its hierarchical structure of reality with immaterial things still having power over material things. The mind still has power over the body. The body is still that which serves, and needs to be controlled by, the mind.

So far I've described how the Christian ontology has existed in at least two forms: 1) medieval supernatural Christianity's three part hierarchical system of spirit – mind – body, where spirit represents both God, the creator, and the human spirit, and 2) modern Christianity's three part hierarchical system of spirit as distant creator of: self – mind – body. Because of the challenge of science, modern Christianity has had to recognize the validity of the natural hierarchy or psychology's three part system of self – mind – body, but it has not given up the notion of God as creator or the soul as the spirit in the body. The difficulty for Christianity is to distinguish clearly the difference between the soul and the mind. Psychology simply collapses the soul into the mind in the form of the self. In other words, the spiritual aspect of human beings has virtually lost its divine connection and has become psychologized. The soul as a being that continues on after death has taken on the status of an article of faith rather than an active part of the human being in the world. Fewer and fewer Christians today are frightened by the threat of eternal damnation.

In order to understand theistic realism in its experiential form, the supernatural must be reduced to the natural. God, the soul, and other supernatural entities must be understood experientially. To the extent that these beings are held to be super-experiential, they are criticized as being meta-experiential constructs. A proper elaboration of this contention must wait until the experientialist philosophy is explicated. But that doesn't keep us from re-forming our understanding of the history of philosophy so as to get a clearer understanding of experientialism. To this end, we can re-direct our thinking to modern philosophy, science, and the development of more rationalistic, relativistic ontologies.

Underlying the various objective realisms, prior to Descartes and the development of science, was the ever-present relativism of many personal or individual realities. All objective realisms not only fought with each other so one could convince or impose one's reality upon the other, and hence, confirm the validity of one's own brand of realism, but they also fought amongst themselves. Conflicts would arise within each camp, and they had to be dealt with. Sometimes they were put down by the infliction of pain or death; sometimes dissidents broke away from the camp and formed their own objective realism; but never to my knowledge has anyone in the Western tradition fundamentally transformed objective realism until Descartes.

Relativistically and humanistically, theological realism is nothing more than the few dominating the many. Since relativism holds that there are as many realities as there are people, and that all of these realities are right, then in a world of apparent objective realisms it is just a matter of whose reality is going to dominate at any given time. Here we look to the clergy of the various objective realisms. For in theological realisms that are based on a sacred book or scriptures someone is needed to edit and interpret these books. It is usually left to the clergy to perform these tasks. Prior to Descartes and the development of science, the few clergy dominated the many in determining what was real, and conflicts were settled through power, oppression, ex-communication, threats of damnation, and other hierarchically determined mental and physical forms of punishment.

As natural philosophers (pre-scientists) began to undermine theology's account of creation and human beings' place in it, the supernatural reality of God was also being undermined, a process still going on today. Since most of contemporary philosophy does not claim adherence to the supernatural existence of God, nor to any supernatural existences; and since science generally rejects the supernatural existence of God; and because the supernatural existence of God as held by many, but by no means all theists, is not compatible with the experientialist philosophy I wish to develop, I want to reframe supernatural existence within the structure of experience. In doing so, I will necessarily have to 'reduce' the supernatural to the experiential, but such a reduction, I believe, will not undermine the relevance of supernatural beliefs, but only keep them from becoming more than they are.

Psychology has already re-framed the supernatural three-part ontology (spirit – mind – body) into another three-part ontology (self – mind – body). In effect, the self represents that aspect of God's nature that either inhabits the body (mind-oriented psychology) or arises from the workings of the brain (body-oriented psychology); it replaces the medieval human spirit. The mind is equated with the mental functions of thinking, cogitating, calculating, reasoning, etc., and the body is equated with anatomy and physiology and the material workings of nature (chemistry and physics).

Experientialism brings the idea and/or experience of God into the structure of experience. And since experience is not constituted by any supernatural component, God and supernatural things will have to be understood in experiential terms. I will argue that God and the supernatural develop out of experience, and that experience consists of the rational or mental components of cognition, affect, and the "I" and the realistic or material components of sensation, behavior, and the environment (physical world). The supernatural will show itself to be the result of experiential interaction. Hopefully, it will become more apparent to the reader why I used both realism and rationalism in the title of this section when I develop the philosophy of experientialism.

4. The Rationalist Challenge

Descartes offered the first potent challenge to realism, especially theistic realism. He was raised in the Catholic tradition and, hence, believed in Christian theistic realism. But he also experienced a good deal of contradiction between what he had learned as a child and what he had come to believe as an adult. The methods of science were beginning to capture people's imaginations. Fundamentally new ways of determining reality were being explored and developed. Ontology (or reality) was becoming human-centered as opposed to the God-centeredness of medieval theistic realism. Human beings, rather than God, were coming to see themselves as ultimate determiners of reality. The human mind was expanding its power to determine reality by integrating the human spirit's capacity to understand abstract entities with its capacity to understand concrete material entities. No longer was a separate ontological capacity of mind (i.e. spirit) needed to explain the phenomena of God and soul.

Descartes argued that the human mind is the ultimate determiner of reality and our only certain basis for knowledge. He doubted the certainty of the senses because the senses can be mistaken. He doubted the certainty of his own body because he could be dreaming and his body could be a phantom. He doubted the certainty of mathematics because a demon could be playing tricks with his mind. But he couldn't doubt that he was doubting. Doubting was a function of his mind, whether or not what he thought matched what he sensed, what he dreamt, or what a demon might put into it. That which was in his mind was his. And he could not doubt his connection to that which was in his mind. Hence, what was in his mind was real (Descartes, 1989).

In locating reality in the human mind, Descartes rejected realism and posited a rationalism. Instead of beings (e.g. God) and physical objects (e.g. trees) coming into the mind as they are, as if the mind were simply an opening for reality to enter, Descartes fixed the human mind as something that always 'intercepts' beings and entities and 'makes them its own'.

At first blush, it looks like Descartes had also rejected traditional objectivism and posited a relativism whereby we cannot get beyond our own minds and into any objective reality. But such was not the case, because when he investigated the contents of his mind to find what was there, he found the objectivism of physical objects and God. He argued that physical objects outside of the mind are not conjured by the mind, but that they exist independently of the mind and produce in the mind the knowledge that they exist outside of the mind. Likewise, he argued that God exists outside of the mind and has implanted in us knowledge of him as existing outside of the mind.

Again, one must ask, is reality one or many? If reality lay in the human mind, and some minds have different, if not contradictory, contents, then are all minds correct? Do all minds possess 'real' reality? Or does the world of beings and objects transcend the mind even though they might have to 'come through' the mind or 'be conditioned' by the mind and, hence, have their reality slightly altered?

Descartes' rationalism forced realism onto a new plane. Prior to Descartes, conflicting realisms fought amongst each other, literally and figuratively, for supremacy. Egyptians fought Jews, Jews fought Christians, Christians fought Arabs, etc. Each group possessed a realistic, objective ontology, but these ontologies were not always compatible. Since realistic objectivism holds that there is but one reality and that that reality exists outside of the mind, and that the mind can reach or grasp that reality, everybody wanted their reality to be that one true reality, or at least come closest to being that one. Descartes made the first attempt to 'level the playing field' upon which all of these conflicting ontologies warred against each other. By relocating reality from outside of the mind to inside of the mind, Descartes put *all* human beings center stage. No longer could a few human beings (e.g. clergy) determine reality for everybody else. All thinking beings could determine reality for themselves.

But Descartes fudged. While he maintained that the human mind is the ultimate determiner of reality, he also maintained that there exist greater realities than the human mind. These greater realities were God and nature. God and nature 'make' the human mind what it is, and, hence, determine its reality. Descartes might have looked inside of his own mind and found God-as-existing-beyond-the-mind, but what happens when an atheist does the same? He (let's say) will not find that idea in his mind. He might find the antithesis of that idea in his mind. A strict relativist will have to affirm that both people are right. Rather than admit that, Descartes affirmed the age old theological realism and, importantly, natural realism. But he did this on a whole new playing field. That new playing field included the human mind. It is the human mind that informs us that God-exists-beyond-the-mind and that nature-exists-beyond-the-mind.

Kant knew that Descartes fudged and he proceeded to develop a 'hermetically sealed' rationalism. Kant argued that we cannot 'get to' or understand the world outside of the mind as it is, because we cannot get outside of our minds (Kant, 1902). Since the only way we can understand the world outside of our minds is with our minds, then it follows that reality is only that which our minds disclose. Hence, a true study of reality is a study of mind. And that is what Kant gives us in his three *Critiques*: 1) *Critique of Pure Reason* is an explication of the structure of the mind in relation to the physical world outside of the mind, 2) *Critique of Practical Reason* is an explication of the structure of the mind in relation to ethics and human organization, and 3) *Critique of Aesthetic Judgment* is an explication of the structure of the mind in relation to the world of art and beauty. In each work, Kant seeks to show how the world outside of the mind is virtually impenetrable. The mind *always* gets in the way of our contact with the world outside of itself. *Everything* is conditioned by the mind, except, of course, the mind itself.

Kant took Descartes' initial attempt to unseat theistic realism and replaced it with a hermetically sealed rationalism. In locating space, time, substance, causation, etc. within the human mind, Kant divested God and nature of their objectivizing power. Descartes couldn't rid himself of the overwhelming idea that God and nature exist independently of his own mind without lying to himself. So he kept the idea that God and nature existed independently of his mind and that it was possible to reach or understand that world on its own terms. This not only made it possible for him to publish his work under the scrutiny and power of the Church, but it also set the scene for the development of science. Establishing nature as that upon which the human mind depends opens the door for a fundamentally new objective realism: science. Kant virtually took theistic realism out of the picture by establishing a strong rationalism, but he was not able to take nature out of the picture. Modern philosophy developed alongside materialistic science, having shucked the confines of theological realism.

I am purposefully using the term "rationalism" to apply to Kant rather than "idealism", which is often applied to him in the literature, because I want to develop a history of ontological development based on the dualism of mind and body. I will understand idealism as a type of rationalism, but not rationalism as a type of idealism. In other words, I am using the term "rationalism" as a broad fundamental ontological category to represent all mind-based ontologies, and I am using the term "realism" to represent all body-based ontologies. Hopefully, my reasons for doing so will become apparent as this work develops.

5. The Transition from Supernaturalism to Naturalism

There are two aspects of human experience that carry with them 'objectivizing power': God (mind) and nature (matter). By 'objectivizing power', I mean the tendency for people to experience certain things as objectively real or independent of any human mind, e.g. God and nature. As science and its method of validating the 'objectively real' developed and gained adherents, the objective reality of God and other things supernatural was seriously challenged. It is much easier to validate the existence of natural things than it is to validate the existence of immaterial beings. Two people looking at an average glass of water might more readily agree upon what exists than they would in regard to a religious service that they both are attending. Both would tend to experience the objective reality of the glass of water, whereas both need not affirm the objective reality in regard to the church service.

So when Descartes relocated the determiner of reality from the supernatural world to the natural mind, he led the way to removing God as the ultimate authority of reality by substituting something that was, perhaps, less difficult to validate than God but still more difficult to validate than the physical world: ideas. If God and things supernatural are divested of their objective reality as supernatural beings but kept as objective realities in the mind, then we alter the plane of objective reality so that more people can determine the workings of that reality for themselves. Locating the power to determine reality in all people's minds and taking that power away from the elite few (clergy) served to collapse the supernatural world into the natural, opening the door for the development of empirical science.

Once the fear of God was dispelled from one's experience, one was free to approach reality in different ways. Since the physical world seemed to offer the broadest possible avenue for validation by others, it seemed to be a good place to start. In this sense, Descartes' rationalism served not only as a way to transfer the locus of power to determine reality from the supernatural to the natural, but it also bridged the gap between the supernatural and the material. Kant's rationalism finished the job started by Descartes by collapsing the supernatural into the natural and expanding the power of the mind in determining objective reality. If we were to find God in Kant's system, he would have to be conditioned by the human mind. The rationalist challenge paved the way for the development of empirical science. It freed human beings from the hierarchically organized grip of supernatural forces and allowed them to utilize their natural minds to understand the natural world around them and themselves in relation to it. The body, which had been an object to be controlled and tamed by the mind, became an object of study. It, along with the objects of the natural world outside of the mind, became the most verifiable form of reality available. People could see what they were talking about, observe how these physical objects move in relation to each other, and apply their rational capacities to form hypotheses and theories about them. The more this was done, the more success people had in understanding and manipulating nature. The more success they had, the more objective their determinations seemed. Their successes only added to the already strong 'objectivizing power' of the physical world.

6. The Empirical Transformation

Rationalism's attack on theistic realism served to diminish the controlling grip of supernaturalism and to open the door for the development of naturalism. Nature was conceived even by theistic realism to be composed of a different substance from the supernatural. That substance was matter. Though the term "matter" has undergone changes in physics as Einsteinian relativity and Quantum physics continue to replace Newtonian physics, for our purposes, I will use "matter" to mean the traditional conception of particles (sub-atomic particles, atoms) that take up space. I will also equate the term "matter" with the term "body" and try to keep my terminology consistent.

The rationalism underlying theistic realism maintained that there are such things as innate ideas. Our idea of God was argued to be the most fundamental innate idea there was. Locke criticized innate ideas by introducing developmental ideas into philosophical discourse (Locke, 1959). No longer were philosophers to create ontologies based solely on adult reasoning. Locke sought to debunk the notion of innate ideas in part by pointing out how children differ from adults.

14

He noticed no such thing as an innate idea of God in children. Rather, he argued that children had to be taught about God. He also argued that not all cultures or people believe in God and those that do often differ in their conceptions of God. In arguing for the relativistic nature of the idea of God and other 'innate' notions, Locke not only attacked theistic realism but also its rationalistic foundation. He took God not only out of heaven but out of the human mind as well.

Where did our knowledge of God come from if not from God (medieval Christianity) or our own minds (rationalism)? With Locke, the rationalism of Descartes shifted to the materialism of science via a synthesis of realistic and rationalistic philosophy.

Empiricism (as well as materialism) is the philosophy underlying science. Natural philosophers (early scientists) coming out of the conflict between theistic realism and humanistic rationalism adopted both "isms" by synthesizing them into a new "ism." Empiricism is realistic in that it accepts the objects that exist outside of the mind as having natures of their own and that are, in this sense, self-subsistent. They, for the most part, do not need the existence of human beings for their existence. How these objects subsist is a matter of some debate, but the huge bulk of empiricists lean toward the Lockean materialistic form of realism rather than the Berkeleyan idealistic (or rationalistic) form. Therefore, I will use the term "empiricism" to refer primarily to materialistic empiricism.

But empiricism is also rationalistic in that it accepts the Kantian thesis that we can never understand objects as they are. Empiricists therefore construct a correspondence theory of reality where they continuously seek to match their mental understanding of the world with the physical reality of that world.

But many scientists allow themselves to slide into a naïve realism and 'forget' that their minds are always conditioning those objects ('objectivizing power'). This tendency to 'forget' the relevance of their minds seems to be so far-reaching in practice that many scientists tend to assume that scientific facts are actually objective entities and not a necessary combination of the mental and the physical. This lack of critical thinking admits of an uncritical presentation of an objective world. The empirical synthesis is distorted. The rationalistic component is covered over by the realistic component, and the latter is tacitly, if not explicitly, assumed to be the 'real' reality. So empiricism, though essentially composed of an ideological paradox, tends to show itself and even understand itself as a new form or realism.

Rationalism reversed the assumptions of realism, but it did not eliminate realism. Science, generally, does what Descartes did. It accepts that the mind will always condition reality outside of the mind, but having accepted that, it 'forgets' it and assumes that the reality that exists outside of the mind is more real than the reality in the mind. Descartes was roundly criticized for doing this by the more consistent rationalists (e.g. Kant), but this was not enough to rid the new empiricism of its realistic bias. Without the rationalistic foundation that theistic realism supplied, empiricists were left to shift their foundation of reality from supernatural immaterialism to natural materialism, and the 'objectifying power' of realism found expression in the other substance, i.e. matter (body).

This flaw is understandable if we look at the certainty we experience in relation to the existence of objects outside of our minds. Descartes, scientists, and people in general tend overwhelmingly to experience objects outside of their minds as objective. How do we account for this fact? How do these objects exist without our being there to see them or interact with them? Materialism supplies an answer: they are made of something that can exist independently of us. And when this idea is extended to the human body, we have the materialistic basis of all reality.

With matter as the only substance comprising reality, the rationalistic element of empiricism is easily 'forgotten'. Science, in general, disregards the existence of the mind as scientists go about their business. So when science 'discovers' new objects, or develops new theories or laws, it forgets that their discoveries are actually renderings of their own minds in conjunction with the physical world. And by "renderings" I do not mean fictional accounts. The 'objectivizing power' of realism is strong and is experienced to be fundamentally different from experiences of fiction, so scientists would tend to deny that their understandings, laws and theories are mere fictional accounts. Yet there is a nagging element of fiction in them. This element is the rationalist component of empiricism. Denying the existence of the mind's part in determining reality, whether tacitly or explicitly, distorts the empiricist transformation of the realist: rationalist dichotomy.

Berkeley rejected materialistic empiricism and sought to re-establish theistic realism in conjunction with empiricism. He argued that all objects considered material are actually combinations of ideas (Berkeley, 1988). That is, when we interact with a ball, we see its shape, size, and color, feel its texture, etc. If all these sense data were to be eliminated, then the ball would disappear. In other words, the only way a human being can know a physical object outside of his mind is via sense data. Therefore, it is the sense data that exist, not matter. And when he tried to account for his knowledge that these objects exist independently of his interacting with them, he offered that these sensual ideas are in the mind of God. Hence, the objects will exist when we aren't around to experience them.

Berkeley's idealistic empiricism sought not only to counter the power of a growing materialistic empiricism but also to re-establish a theistic, supernatural realism. But Berkeley didn't need God to account for what psychologists refer to as object constancy or object permanence. He could have argued a straight rationalist thesis that holds that we know that physical objects remain in tact when we are not interacting with them because that knowledge is in our minds. Our minds 'tell us' that some objects are permanent. Whether or not the object actually is in tact when we are not experientially connected to it is impossible to prove. We can only prove the existence of that with which we are in some way in contact. This latter notion is more consistent with quantum physics, and it doesn't require a return to supernatural theism to support itself.

7. The Phenomenological and Pragmatic Transformations

The battle between realism and rationalism continued into the nineteen and twentieth centuries. Hegel accepted the rationalist thesis that the mind conditions everything outside of the mind, but he rejected Kant's hermetically sealed form of rationalism. Hegel couldn't accept the logical conclusion that Kant's rationalism forced us to draw, i.e. that the only legitimate study of reality is the study of the human mind. He understood the mind to be one aspect of reality and objects outside of the mind to be another aspect. In other words, if we are to talk reality at all, we have to include both mind and matter. Reality, for Hegel and the phenomenologists that followed, is composed of mental and physical phenomena as opposed to mental ideas and physical objects. Thoughts and feelings are mental phenomena, while bodies and objects in nature are physical phenomena. Both sets of phenomena are necessary if we are going to talk meaningfully about reality (Hegel, 1977).

But Hegel moved away from trying to legitimize the reality of matter and placed both things of the mind and things of matter within an overarching spirit. Mind and matter became manifestations of spirit. In Hegel, rationalism won out over realism. Idealism contextualized materialism.

Shortly after Hegel, Husserl advanced the theory of intentionality which held that consciousness is consciousness-of-something (Husserl, 1931). By this he meant that when we are conscious, we have to be conscious of something, whether that something is mental (thoughts, feelings) or physical (bodies, objects). This theory linked inextricably the human mind with an object of some sort. Pure consciousness was impossible. Consciousness always came with an object. Pure materiality was inconsequential because human beings had to have some sort of contact with a material object in order to talk about its existence. Whether or not something existed independently of our experience of it was inconsequential. In short, reality, for the phenomenologists, was that which is real-for-us.

Husserl's phenomenology also forced a synthesis of the real and the rational. No longer were we to understand reality as dual in nature, i.e. mind vs. matter (or body). Rather, reality was singular; it was composed of phenomena. And these phenomena came in two types, mental and physical. But in order for Husserl to maintain that mental phenomena could be objects of consciousness, he had to split consciousness into that which is conscious (ego) and that which is the object of consciousness (idea, feeling, etc.) When he did this, he opened the door for a continuation of the battle between the rational and the real. Just like theistic realism split mind into spirit and mind, phenomenology split mind into transcendent ego and object of consciousness, whether that object is mental or physical. This created two distinct ontological worlds, though as subsets within one phenomenological world. Just like Hegel did in arguing for the equality of existence between mental and physical phenomena only to 'break form' and assert that both mental things and physical things are part of a bigger system (spirit), Husserl argued for the equality of mental and physical phenomena, only to 'break form' and assert that the essence of any mental or physical phenomenon lay in the mind. For instance, if an equality-oriented phenomenologist were to study a physical object that he (let's say) was not familiar with, he would seek to describe its appearance and movements as best he could. This relationship looks like this: "I"— [consciousness – object], where the "I" represents that which is conscious and [consciousness – object] represents the inextricable connection between consciousness and an object of consciousness. When looking at a physical object, the "I" could be neglected or overlooked. The researcher would be interested in the object and lose sight of the functioning "I" (just like material empiricists lose sight of the function of their own minds when studying a physical thing), but when the "I" is 'looking at' a thought, an idea, or a feelings then its function is hard to overlook. When studying the contents of our own minds, we seem to be forced to recognize the existence of that which is 'looking at' or studying those mental contents. The 'that' which is studying is, for Husserl, the transcendent ego. Once it is admitted that there is a transcendent ego studying the mental contents of one's own mind, then we have an ontology that is constituted by two distinct components: transcendent ego and [consciousness – object]. Positing the existence of a transcendent ego puts the phenomenologists back into the dualistic ballpark. Now there exists a mental or mind phenomenon (ego) that studies mental objects (ideas, feelings) and physical objects (body, objects in nature), and we're back where we started from, though on a fundamentally different plane. Now the question is: in which area does reality lie, the transcendent ego or the object of consciousness?

Husserl eventually gave way to the 'objectivizing power' of God (or the rational), just as Hegel had done. The continental European bias toward the rational became evident when Husserl located essences (the 'real' phenomena) in the mind and awarded physical objects necessary but not sufficient ontological status. His transcendental phenomenology affirmed the superiority of rationalistic reality at the expense of the realistic.

EXPERIENTIALISM

To counter Husserl's rationalist bias, existential phenomenologists like Sartre and Heidegger denied the existence of a
transcendent "I". Sartre said in effect that when we study a physical
or mental phenomenon, we engage in a series of experiences, some
that are constituted with the "I" and some that are not. For instance,
when we study a physical object and are not aware of the fact that we
are studying that object, our consciousness is non-self-reflective. We
are "into" what we are studying. When we study our own mental
contents, we are equally absorbed in the enterprise. It doesn't matter
if the object of consciousness is mental or physical; there is no "I" in
either of these consciousnesses. But when we reflect upon ourselves
as studying the physical object or the contents of our minds, then our
consciousness includes the "I". Understanding the "I" as a
component of consciousness at one moment in time (self-reflection)
and not as a component of consciousness at another moment in time
(non-reflection) rids us of the notion of the transcendent ego. There is
no ego that oversees non-reflective and self-reflective experiences but
rather one that goes in and out of consciousness (Sartre, 1957).

While Sartre got rid of the notion of the transcendent ego, he did
not get rid of the notion of essences and the duality of being. He
divided being into the 'for-itself' and the 'in-itself', where the for
itself referred to self-reflective experiences and the in-itself referred
to non-reflective experiences. For example, when we look at a tree
non-reflectively, the tree represents the in-itself of the phenomenon of
the tree. If someone were to ask us what we are doing while we are
looking at the tree, we could reflect upon ourselves looking at the tree
and then tell the person what we are doing. This reflecting upon
ourselves looking at the tree represents the for-itself aspect of being.
The for-itself is constituted by self-reflection and the looking at the
tree. When we reflect upon the image of the tree 'in our head' and
'study' it, we are reflecting upon the in-itself of the cognition.

If this analysis is accurate, then the in-itself of the tree (in nature)
is fundamentally different from the tree as an objective physical
existent (as science mistakenly tends to affirm). And the in-itself of
the image (or cognition) allows the phenomenologist to affirm the
separate though equal existence of mental phenomena (which science
cannot do). But in positing the split existence of the for-itself, Sartre,
like Hegel and Husserl before him, allows for a duality of being. As

per our example, the self-reflective experience consists of self-reflection *and* looking-at-the-tree, or, to simplify: the self *and* looking at the tree. As soon as the self is understood to exist over and against the looking-at-the-tree, the rational is pitted against the real, where the rational is represented by the self and the real is represented by both physical phenomena outside of the mind (e.g. tree) and mental phenomena inside of the mind (e.g. image of the tree). But in Sartre's case, instead of opting for rationalism to be the locus of being (phenomenal essences), he opted for realism.

As applied to our example, the essence of the tree lies not in the tree-as-physical-object (this is naïve science and common sense realism) but in the tree-as-related-to-us. The tree-as-related-to-us is represented in the non-reflective experience of looking at the tree (tree as in-itself) and the self-reflective experience of looking at the tree (tree as for-itself). In both experiences, the looking-at-the-tree is where the phenomenal essence of being (reality) is located, and not in the self, which accompanies the looking-at-the-tree in the self-reflective experience.

When Sartre got rid of the transcendent ego, he was left with the task of locating essences somewhere. Since he got rid of the rationalistic 'power' component, i.e. the ego, he was left with the realistic 'power' component, i.e. the physical phenomenon. He overlooked the rest of the rationalistic component (self) after he extracted the transcendent ego. Just like the scientists who accepted empiricism and then overlooked its rationalistic component, existential phenomenologists like Sartre and Heidegger overlooked the rationalistic component of phenomena and located essence in the things themselves.

The phenomenologists divided themselves up into the same old camps: existential phenomenologists were transformed realistic empiricists and the transcendental phenomenologists were transformed rationalistic empiricists. The synthesis of mind and body, where the mental and physical phenomena were equal in their claims to ontological status, was short-lived. It was overtaken by the realistic:rationalistic bias.

When empiricism tried to synthesize the mind and the body or the rational and the real, it gave lip service to the rationalistic aspect of the combination and acted as if the realistic aspect were the only reality. Allying itself with materialism, empiricism forced its rationalistic element into the background, sometimes so far into the background that it was denied, even while it was operating within the minds of scientists. Materialism, equipped with a heavy dose of 'objectivizing power' began to account for rationalistic components (thoughts, ideas) by reducing them to forms of matter. Science accepted the Cartesian circle as consistent and real. Phenomenology picked up the torch that empiricism dropped and forced a synthesis of the mind and the body, the mental and the physical (or material). It allotted equal reality to both things mental and physical. Husserl believed that he had developed a new, more inclusive, science, the science of phenomena (Husserl, 1931).

Pierce, James and Dewey did the same thing in America that Hegel and Husserl did in Europe. Pragmatism (or what James called a radical empiricism) sought to elevate the reality of the forgotten rationalism constituting materialistic empiricism. The pragmatists maintained that the mind cannot be eliminated from reality or derived from another reality (matter) but that both mind and matter were needed to discuss reality at all; mind and matter were two sides of the same reality coin. Their acid test of reality was "does it work," or does the combination of things mental and physical work together in a whole (James, 1981).

While Continental European philosophy centered on the rationalistic aspect of reality, seeking essences, whether mind-based or body (matter)-based, the American philosophy of pragmatism centered on the materialistic aspect. James could not get rid of metaphysics like the materialistic empiricists and analytic philosophers sought to do. He could not accept the narrow limitations of materialistic science. But neither could he admit to the existence of rationalistic essences. So the pragmatists, like the phenomenologists, transformed reality into a necessary combination of the mental and the physical and used practical coherence of the various and sundry systems (combinations) to elevate pragmatic realities above pure relativism. Not everyone's reality was equally 'real', but rather those realties that combine rationalistic (mental) and realistic (physical) aspects into a coherent whole had greater claim to reality.

Both philosophies transformed idealistic and materialistic empiricism in the same way empiricism transformed realism and rationalism. They just did it from opposing ends. Continental philosophy sought to raise the reality status of matter and the body, and American pragmatism sought to raise the status of the mental and the mind. James included religious experience as legitimate ontology, whereas his empirical cohorts tended to reject all forms of the supernatural from the status of reality. Sartre eliminated the transcendent ego and located essential being (essences) in the things themselves instead of locating them within the mind (Husserl) or an overarching spirit (Hegel). But the 'objectivizing power' of the dual nature of reality, of the mind and the body, the mental and the physical, kept re-asserting itself every time an integration of the two was attempted.

Viewed from the perspective of a battle between the mind and the body or the mental and the physical for ontological supremacy, the history of philosophy (and all other areas of human life) could be understood as a recognition of two opposing worlds that have been trying, paradoxically, to integrate themselves as they sought to establish supremacy over each other. Viewed from this perspective, the era of supernatural realism (ancient and medieval eras) consisted of the supremacy of the mind over the body, though the mind was split into two components, the natural and the supernatural, where the supernatural controlled the whole system. When science started debunking long held religious ideas, the reified mind of the supernatural eventually collapsed into the mind proper and became the "self" of psychology. Once the supernatural was made natural, the mind qua mind and the body continued their fight for supremacy though without the supernatural distortions. The mind in Continental Europe held on to its supremacy in the face of a growing materialistic science through Descartes' and Kant's rationalism, which served to raise the legitimacy of the natural mind over against the supernatural mind while it countered the growing strength of materialism. The body (matter) of Anglo-America and Russia held on to its supremacy in the face of a still strong reified rationalism (supernaturalism) and a growing natural rationalism, but it couldn't get rid of natural rationalism no matter how hard it tried. Pragmatism attempted to reestablish the ontological legitimacy of the mind within a materialistic framework.

8. A Brief Summary

Though empiricism succeeded initially in synthesizing rationalism and realism, it split itself into materialistic and rationalistic camps. The materialistic camp consisted of Locke and Hume's materialistic-leaning empiricism and the rationalistic camp consisted of Berkeley's rationalistic-leaning empiricism. Though the dualism of mind and body integrated itself as separate but equal realities by ridding rationalism of its supernatural distortion, it could not integrate natural rationalism with natural materialism. The 'objectivizing power' of each ontological area was too strongly opposed to each other.

Though natural rationalism succeeded in integrating supernatural realism with rationalism by collapsing the supernatural into the natural, it did not succeed in swallowing up realism. Realism just shifted its weight from supernatural realism to materialism. So when empiricism synthesized the rational with the real, it did so by synthesizing the mental with the material. But the strength of the materialist aspect of this dual ontology had been winning out in practice, so much so that pragmatism had to counter it in an attempt to once again even the playing field and re-establish the rationalist component.

Though natural rationalism succeeded in countering the power of a growing materialistic empiricism, which was more accurately, I think, a naïve realism, through the work of Kant, it eventually had to give way to the new influx of realism in the form of Hegelian phenomenology. Kant could not eliminate the power of the body (matter) no matter how hard he tried. Hegel brought it back in his phenomenology, changing realism to include both mental and physical phenomena. Ontology was once again transformed to another level.

The underlying power of integration would not let either rationalism (mind) or realism (body) win out over the other. Kant's rationalism tried to eliminate materialism altogether, and it failed. Materialistic empiricism, analytic philosophy and positivism tried to eliminate rationalism altogether, but it failed. Neither side would permit the other side to swallow it up. And both sides tried to integrate themselves with each other, first through the empirical synthesis, and later though the phenomenological/pragmatic synthesis. But both of these attempts at synthesis failed as the 'objectivizing power' of each camp asserted itself in the mind:body developments within the synthesized ontological structure.

What I hope to offer in the following pages is a third attempt at synthesizing mind and body, the mental with the physical, and the many with the one. This time I trust that the synthesis will 'take' and form an actual integration of mind and body, equalizing the power of the mental with the physical, and uniting the many with the one in one ontological structure. I certainly cannot guarantee its success, but I certainly cannot deny in myself the need to try.

PART 2: Experientialism

1. The Structure of Experience: A Definition

In attempting to integrate the mind & the body, the mental & the physical, and the many & the one, beyond the historical efforts that have already taken place, I have found it necessary to develop a fundamentally new perspective and to re-organize our current vocabularies to fit this perspective. In doing so, I certainly do not wish to disregard the 'isms' and 'ologies' above or to fail to recognize my great debt to them and those who developed them. It is out of a profound respect for the power of realism and rationalism and for all those who sought to integrate them that I offer this work.

Experientialism maintains that experience equals reality, and that experience is constituted by six components: cognition, affect, behavior, sensation, the environment, and the "I". Consciousness, on the other hand, is constituted by five components: cognition, affect, behavior, sensation, and the environment. This distinction is heuristic rather then ontological. Whether or not we maintain that consciousness exists prior to experience and that experience is ultimately 'founded upon' consciousness is of little concern, because it is only out of experience that we can make the claim that consciousness precedes experience. It is only out of experience that we can make any objective claim at all.

Cognition refers to all the thoughts, ideas, images, under-standings, cogitations, calculations, etc. that go through our minds.

Affect refers to feelings, emotions, and moods. Behavior refers to our bodies in motion, whether that motion is internal as in physiology or external as in comportment. Sensation refers to the functioning of our five senses (seeing, hearing, etc.). Environment refers to the world around us, including our own bodies. And the "I" refers to the function of ownership, i.e. *my* thought, *my* feeling, *my* behavior, *my* sensation, and *my* environment/body.

2. The Interdependence of Components of Experience

All of these components are necessary if experience is to exist. If one of these components were to be eliminated, all would be eliminated. For example, if environment were to be eliminated, then there would be no world around us: no people, no objects, no earth, no air, no space, and no physical body. There would just be 'us', whatever 'us' might be.

Supernatural realism offers that there would exist a soul, i.e. a disembodied existent, among other disembodied existents, perhaps in a non-physical place where souls can congregate, i.e. heaven. But the problem with this notion, aside from our inability to verify souls and heaven sensually, is that any such belief is part-and-parcel experiential. Whether or not there actually are souls or a heaven is of absolutely no consequence, because we cannot get out of the experiential structures within which we participate to grasp this 'objective' reality.

For example, if I were to maintain that my soul will continue on after my death, then the experience within which I participate would look like this:

Cognition: My soul will continue on after I die
Affect: confidence
Behavior: talking
Sensation: other person
Environ: room
"I":   ownership

If I were then asked to prove this to someone who did not understand or agree with me, then I might refer to the Bible for support. But such a referral would look like this:
Cognition: It says in Revelations....

Affect: increased confidence
Behavior: looking at Bible
Sensation: Bible
Environment: room
"I":   ownership

I would still be *in* the experiential structure. Simply because I refer to a book that is held by some people to be the authoritative word of God does not mean that I have somehow transcended experience. Nor, simply because my confidence increases the more I quote from that book, does it mean that I am closer to any absolute objective reality-beyond-experience. It merely means that I am very confident in what I am saying.

So when responding to the supernatural realist, the experientialist might re-frame the supernaturalist's claim and place it in experience, and keep it there.

Another argument against the idea that removing the environment from consciousness eliminates consciousness comes from transcendental meditators. Transcendental meditators will maintain that they can reach a state of pure consciousness by eliminating the environment from consciousness without becoming unconscious.

An argument against that notion is that they might have reduced consciousness of the environment to a minimum, but they have not been able to remove themselves completely from the environment. If the environment impinges upon them strongly enough, then they will be aware of it (e.g. drilling into their tooth to the nerve).

Another argument against this notion comes from science and the assumptions underlying empiricism and materialism. The argument maintains that consciousness is the product of neuron activity in the brain. If activity reaches a certain level, then we are considered to be conscious. For instance, the awake state of being more often than not indicates that a person is conscious because brain activity is strong. But science will also maintain that REM (rapid eye movement) sleep is also indicative of consciousness because the brain activity is sufficient to meet the materialistic criterion for consciousness. But once the brain activity slips below REM sleep, then the person will be considered unconscious.

It follows from this definition of consciousness that when a person dies and all brain activity ceases, then consciousness is eliminated, at least for that individual. If all conscious beings on the earth were to die, and all brain activity ceased, then consciousness would be eliminated from the planet. But life or existence of other things would go on.

Though this is a huge topic for philosophical discussion, I will, per the essential nature of this work, address it briefly. If we cannot remove ourselves from the experiential structures within which we participate, then any belief we might have that the environment continues on while we are unconscious or after we die is simply that: a belief. We infer in consciousness that we were asleep because things around us, as well as ourselves, have changed. We also infer that since people around us have died and life still goes on that when we die life will go on. Whether or not life (and non-living beings) exist while we are asleep or dead is of absolutely no consequence to us. Only in experience do unconscious and dead states of being matter to us.

Another argument against the inclusion of the environment in consciousness comes from the history of philosophy and common sense: *we* are conscious beings, aware of our environments and aware of ourselves in our environments; *we* are separate from our environment; our environment is physical in nature; *we* are mental, spiritual, non-mental; the mental interacts with the physical, but it does not need the physical in order to be; the physical impinges upon the mental, but the physical does not need the mental in order to be.

Part of this idea overlaps with the empirical/materialist argument and can be dealt with in a similar manner: most people understand that physical objects in the world exist whether or not we perceive them, but simply because we understand them to exist in this manner doesn't mean that they 'do' exist in this manner. Some of these objects might cease to exist when we are not perceiving them. Psychologists will argue that infants do not experience objects of perception as constant until their brains and their interaction with their environments develop to the stage of achieving object constancy or object permanence. Prior to reaching this stage, objects seem to pop in and out of existence. If this experience persisted and no people ever experienced object constancy, then our understanding of the world would be vastly different from the one we currently have.

EXPERIENTIALISM

From the experiential point of view, the question is not whether or not the physical world continues on when we are asleep or dead or that it has an existence of its own, separate from people's connection to it; the question is "what difference would it make if it did or did not have an existence of its own?" As long as we experience it to have an existence of its own, then that is what is important. Whether it 'really' has an existence of its own is of no consequence to us.

The other part of the above argument can be responded to in this manner: materialistic science is arguing for the reduction of the mental and the spiritual to the physical, that things mental are fabrications and are actually neuron activity in the brain. Briefly, the experiential rebuttal is that no scientist can remove him or herself from the experiential structures within which he or she participates even to conceive of such an idea, let alone prove it to be 'true'. Cognition will always be cognition; it is not reducible to matter (brain activity). Even if the materialist were to perceive his own brain activity through special goggles, then it is the brain activity that is perceived and not the thought. The brain activity is "believed" to be the thought. We will discuss materialism at more length in Part 3 of this book.

If sensations were to be eliminated from experience, then we would not be able to see, hear, taste, smell or feel anything. If there existed an environment for us to be in contact with, we would not know it because there would be no way for us to be in contact with it.

This idea is challenged by people who have done work with sensory deprivation tanks. They contend that when people are cut off from all sensory input they will tend to hallucinate. This is supposed to indicate that sensory input is not necessary for there to be cognitive functioning.

In rebuttal to this challenge, it could be argued that the people in sensory deprivation tanks might have their sensory input greatly diminished, and this diminishment might prompt them to hallucinate as a form of compensation, but this does not mean that they have successfully eliminated all sensory input.

Also, if all sensory input were to be eliminated from conception on, then what would we be conscious of? Our own thought? Thoughts of what?

Another argument against this notion comes from neuroscientists who maintain that neuron activity in the brain occurs when we are not in immediate contact with that which we are "sensing". For instance, we can process dream material without being in contact with the objects of our dreams.

This argument is rebutted by arguing that dream material is derived from previous experiences, either direct or indirect (e.g. pictures, stories, etc.) and synthesized into an imaginative dream format. The brain activity would not occur if there were no sensory input into the organism from conception on. The brain activity accesses a stockpile of past sensory data and imaginative connections and this data can be processed in the imagination without any direct contact with objects in the environment.

If we eliminate the behavioral component of consciousness, then we would not be aware of any physiological activity within our body or that our body is comporting itself within an environment. In effect, we would be unconscious or dead.

Arguments against this idea can easily be found in our beliefs about, and empirical evidence for, unconscious states of being. We are not aware of physiological activity or our bodily comportment if we are asleep or in some other unconscious state, and yet we exist. Therefore, ontology includes conscious and unconscious states of being. Hence, that which is real must be something more than experience; it must be something that includes experience as a part of existence.

The argument against this notion is that any claims we make about unconscious states are made consciously. We know that there are unconscious states of being because we infer from observation of others and possibly ourselves if videotaped that such states exist. We also infer that we must have been unconscious if the last thing we remember while conscious differed significantly from what we experience now; things have changed. But in both of these instances, it is the inference that is real. Whether or not there exist unconscious states beyond experience is wholly inconsequential.

If we eliminate the affective component of experience, then we would be reduced to automatons or machines. We could think without feeling anything in relation to our thinking, i.e. no interest, no excitement, no boredom, no apathy, no confidence, no indifference. In effect, we would not be human.

Materialistic science offers the strongest argument I know against this claim. For if everything is made out of matter, then it follows that feelings are made out of matter. Science has identified the limbic system of the brain as the center for feelings and various neurotransmitters as causally related to the existence of feelings. It posits that stimuli from outside and inside the human organism will cause a response from the nervous system, which will then stimulate other areas of the body, and cause a variety of behaviors that will, in turn, affect the environment; and the deterministic cause-and-effect chain continues indefinitely.

We will deal extensively with science's contentions throughout this work. Suffice it to say right now that experientialism will argue that to the extent that science reduces feelings and emotions to the workings of matter, it disregards the existence of the feelings and emotions that drive the very work scientists do; it skews experience toward its environmental component, and hence it provides us with a distorted version of reality, unless that version can be owned by the scientists promoting it.

If we eliminate the cognitive component from consciousness, we would not be able to understand anything about the world around us or the world inside us. We would, in effect, be unconscious or dead. Again, science offers a strong argument against this idea, not because the total elimination of brain activity would be equivalent to death, and in death there is no consciousness, but because science's materialistic basis does not support the experientialist contention that experience equals reality. For science, reality is something independent, as well as constitutive, of the human mind. Cognition is reduced to the material functioning of the brain and other related biological entities. Hence, if the brain ceases to function, then we are not conscious. We are, in effect, dead.

Again, the experientialist argument in relation to science will be developed throughout this entire work. The extent to which science reduces cognition to electro-chemical activity in the brain is the extent to which it disregards the thoughts and ideas that direct the very work scientists do. When cognition is reduced to matter in motion, and not owned as a cognition in itself, then experience is skewed and reality is distorted.

3. A Meta-Experiential Construct

When a creationist claims that God created and sustains the world, she (let's say) is making an objective claim. She is claiming that this is so not only for her but for everybody, whether everybody believes this or not. When an evolutionist claims that the universe started with the Big Bang and develops and changes through natural selection, he (let's say) is also making an objective claim. Both the creationist and the evolutionist are claiming that the experience within which they are participating exists because of some causes other than experience itself, i.e. that their very claims are the product of processes other than the experience within which their claim exists.

When asked to support or prove her claim, a creationist might quote the Bible, disclose personal experience, relay testimony, give a rational argument, etc. When asked to support or prove his claim, an evolutionist might convey claims from geology, paleontology, comparative anatomy, etc. These sets of experiences might look like this:

Creationist

Cognition:	God created the world and us
Affect:	confidence
Behavior:	talking
Sensation:	other person
Environ:	room
"I":	ownership

which is replaced by:

Cognition:	bible quote
Affect:	increased confidence
Behavior:	reading
Sensation:	bible
Environ:	room
"I":	ownership

Evolutionist

Cognition:	We and the universe evolved from primordial matter
Affect:	confidence

Behavior:	talking
Sensation:	other person
Environ:	room
"I":	ownership

which is replaced by:

Cognition:	Paleontology data
Affect:	increased confidence
Behavior:	reading (from text)
Sensation:	text
Environ:	room
"I":	ownership

Though both creationist and evolutionist are making objective claims, neither of them get outside of their respective experiential structures to make good or prove the objectivity of their claim. And neither of them will ever get outside of the experiential structures within which their claim exists. Any attempt to get out of the structure of experience will land them back in experience. If this is so, then the referent of their respective claims (e.g. an actual God's act of creation and actual matter's evolutionary processes) must be owned [by the experiencer]. It is the creationist's claim that God created the universe; it is the evolutionist's claim that the universe evolved from primordial matter. Whether God 'actually' created the universe, or whether it 'actually' evolved from primordial matter is wholly inconsequential. What *is* consequential is that we believe, hold, are certain of, or have faith in the claims we make.

When someone makes an objective claim and assumes that the reality that supposedly corresponds to his (let's say) claim is somehow greater or more ontologically powerful than his claim itself, then he is creating a meta-experiential construct. A *meta-experiential construct* is a cognition (idea, claim) that is held to correspond with a reality-beyond-experience, a reality that somehow determines, creates, and/or sustains experience itself. But since we cannot get beyond experience to verify this reality, we must hold that every objective cognition that is held to be beyond experience is fundamentally false. It is false not because it does not accurately capture the reality corresponding to the claim; it is false because it assumes that we can get outside of the experiential structure and grasp 'objective' reality.

Objective claims or beliefs are objective inasmuch as they are components of experience. When they are held to transcend experience, then they lose their objectivity and their reality. They become un-realities, types of reified experiences, experiences made into something outside of or beyond them. When we make an objective claim without owning the objectivity of that claim, while maintaining the objectivity of the claim, then we are creating a meta-experiential construct. For instance, when a theist claims that he (let's say) is doing X because it is God's will for him to do X, while not owning the claim, then he is denying ownership of the claim to the degree that he understands himself as a vessel through which God is imparting His will. Likewise, when an evolutionist claims that she (let's say) is doing Y because her genes dispose her to do Y within environment E, while not owning her own claim, then she is creating a meta-experiential construct. In order to avoid the criticism of creating a meta-experiential construct, the creationist and the evolutionist must own the objectivity of their own claims. Their claims can be rendered: My doing X is God's will [for me] and my doing Y is the result of my genetic structure within a certain environment [for me]. Whether or not their objective claims actually "capture" a referent beyond experience is totally inconsequential.

Experientialism, as an ontology, stands as a whole, opposed to the reductionism of materialism, the reductionism of rationalism, and the distorted reductionism of supernatural realism. It seeks neither to replace these ontologies with yet another objectivistic ontology nor to develop a pure relativistic ontology, but to integrate these ontological perspectives into a new ontology that combines relativism and objectivism, where the rational and the real cannot be pulled apart from each other so that one can dominate the other. It seeks to integrate the rational with the real, the mind with the body, and the many with the one, and to refuse the ascendancy of either of them.

4. The Structure of Experience: An Analysis

When we look at a tree, do we see a product of God's creation (supernatural realism), something conditioned entirely by our own mind (rationalism), ideas of extension, size, shape, color, and texture that exist in and independently of our minds (idealism, or rationalistic empiricism), a collection of particles that take up space (materialism), qualities of extension, size, shape, color, and texture that exist in the objects themselves (materialistic empiricism), a phenomenon whose essence lies in the tree's connection to the human mind (existential phenomenology), a phenomenon whose essence lies in the mind's connection to the tree (transcendental phenomenology), or an object that is a part of a coherent combination of physical and mental existents (pragmatism)?

All of these 'isms' and 'ologies' have sought to account for the reality of this tree by positing *other* realities. Supernatural realism posits the reality of God to account for the existence of the tree; rationalism posits the existence of a particularly constituted mind that conditions all physical reality; materialism posits the existence of particles that take up space and move according to their own natures (atoms); empiricism posits the existence of ideas or qualities of objects known through perception or sensation; phenomenology posits essences that inhere within the mind's connection with the object of consciousness or within the object's connection with the mind; pragmatism posits the existence of both mental and physical things combined into a coherent 'world'.

Stated this way, we can trace the development or evolution of mind-body dualism and see how those realities that have been 'added' to the reality of the tree in order to account for the tree's existence reflect a 'coming together' or 'synthesis' of the mental and the physical.

For instance, the early development of supernatural realism fought to reign supreme over all other ontologies (reality structures). To the extent that it succeeded it perpetuated a distorted form of rationalism. The belief that human qualities of power, justice, virtue, knowledge, love, mercy, etc. existed to an infinite degree outside of human beings and within a being wholly independent of them was not held merely to be a belief, i.e. a rationalistic entity. Rather, it was held to be a reality not only independent of human beings and human minds, but also one that created and sustained the existence of human beings. Human beings were dependent upon this reality for their very existence. Such an inversion of rationalism had to be addressed before the mind:body problem or the dualism that underlay supernatural realism could be seen.

Descartes initiated the process of inverting supernatural realism and returning rationalistic components to their rightful owners, i.e. human beings, by founding ultimate reality within the human mind. Kant finished the job that Descartes started by eliminating all possibility of knowing the world around us as it is and confining ultimate reality to the structure of the human mind. The development of Descartes through Kant solidified supernatural realism's return to rationalism. Human beings reclaimed their own qualities. Now rationalism could be seen more clearly as natural rather than supernatural.

But natural rationalism put us in the position of denying our own experience of the world around us, i.e. nature. It forced us to realize that our minds conditioned everything we came into contact with in the world around us, but we couldn't get away from the 'objectivizing power' of realism. We *knew* that the tree we were looking at existed independently of us and had a nature of its own, even though we also knew that the only way we could know the tree we were looking at was through our minds. The two knowledges opposed each other and we were either caught in a logical contradiction or in living a paradox.

With supernatural realism greatly reduced in its power to account for the tree's existence, we were forced to turn our accountings elsewhere. But all of these new accountings were to take place on the plane of naturalism.

Many people argued that the tree existed independently of us because it is made of things that do not need us around for them to function (e.g. atoms). But this notion defied experience also because when people look at a tree they do not see a bunch of atoms traveling around at great speeds, let alone even tinier electrons traveling around the nucleuses of these atoms. To a person not familiar with physics or disposed to thinking in these terms, this notion might seem like science fiction or the product of insanity.

One way to bridge materialism with everyday experience is to posit the existence of sense data: extension (3-dimensionality), size, shape, color, texture, etc. We can 'see' the tree as a three-dimensional object that is a certain size, shape, color, etc. This notion aligns well with everyday experience, and it is a way to keep our minds grounded in the world around us. Even a person who, from time to time, hallucinates a tree will have to admit, during times of lucidity, that the actual tree possesses certain qualities that are 'more real' than the qualities possessed by the hallucinatory tree.

What if one person sees the object one way and another person sees it another way, and neither of them can get out of their way of seeing? The person hallucinating can become lucid and then understand his hallucinations in terms of his lucid experience, but a color-blind person cannot (unless anatomically or physiologically manipulated) see the same quality that a color-seeing person can see. And if the color-blind people in the world greatly outnumbered the color-seeing people, then we might have a slightly different science of color than we currently have. Right now, because the color-seeing people greatly outnumber the color-blind people, the science of color recognizes the existence of certain colors that color-blind people do not. But the reverse also can be argued: that color-blind people recognize the existence of colors that color-seeing people do not. For instance, a color-blind person might see two shades of a particular color whereas a color-seeing person would see the same two colors as quite divergent. Which one is right? Are the colors shades of one color or two distinctly different colors? If neither the color-blind person nor the color-seeing person can get outside of his experience, then the idea that there is an ultimate reality of color and that both of these people cannot be right is fundamentally in error.

Color is certainly not the only quality possessed (or reflected) by objects in the world around us that admits of discrepancy in human experience. A child can experience the house she is living in as 'very big' only to leave the house and return to it as an adult and experience it as 'very small'. The pure (Kantian) rationalist would argue that the size of the house is the product of how the mind conditions it. Unfortunately, Kant's rationalism does not include developmental ideas. Kant's "mind" is an absolute unchanging structure that once and for all conditions the world around us according to its own rules of conditioning, i.e. its categories. This is one reason Hegel rejected the logical conclusions that Kant's rationalism forced upon us and opted to include the realistic component of material reality. This forced Kantian rationalism to deal with materialistic realism. The two realities forged a dialogue that takes place in time. The mind interacts with matter; and matter, in turn, acts upon mind; which, in turn, interacts with matter, etc. This dialogue between mind and matter forced us to think in terms of the passage of time: history. It introduced the notion of development and change into Kant's rationalistic unchanging structure of the mind. Locke's materialistic empiricism already introduced change into ontology by negating the notion of innate ideas and replacing it with learning from experience. So when Darwin came along, he was already disposed to thinking in terms of changing ontology. His theory of evolution followed naturally from this disposition.

Though the empiricist's positing of sense data to account for the reality of a tree helped ground the human mind in 'reality' and gave diverging experiences of physical objects in the world a ground upon which to agree, it was not enough to synthesize mind and body. As long as people don't see things the same way, we are going to have ontological discrepancies. And when change is introduced into ontology, then we have an even greater problem. Now we have to come to agreement on how any given object in the world around us changes. We need to agree not only on the 'anatomy' but the 'physiology' of the 'body'.

From the experientialist point of view, the tree that we are looking at is an integral component of experience. The experience can be rendered thusly:

Cognition: that is a tree
Affect: interest
Behavior: looking at the tree
Sensation: the tree
Environ: outside
"I":   ownership

The tree is an object in our environment that we are sensing and know to be a tree. It is not simply an object that exists independently of our minds that comes into our minds unmodified or unconditioned (realism, materialistic realism, naïve materialistic empiricism). Nor is it something that is the product of the structure of our minds (rationalism, idealism). Rather, it is a component of experience that cannot be separated from the other components of experience.

When we attempt to separate the objects in our environment from experience and posit a reality other than experience to account for them, we distort reality. Experience will not allow us to get outside of itself. Every attempt we make at getting beyond experience and offering up an alternative ground upon which to base experience, we land up back in experience, though we might not know it.

For instance, the scientist who looks at a tree and posits that the tree is made of atoms that are constituted in a particular way, move in a particular way, and interact with each other in a particular way does nothing to get outside of the experiential structures within which he (let's say) participates. Rather, he explains the experience within which he participates (depicted above) by participating in other experiences that bear an explanatory relationship to the original experience. Incredibly oversimplified, this structure could be represented in this fashion:

Cognition:	that is a tree
Affect:	interest
Behavior:	looking at tree
Sensation:	the tree
Environ:	outside
"I":	ownership

which changes to:

Cognition:	It is made of atoms
Affect:	interest
Behavior:	reflectively looking at tree
Sensation:	the tree
Environ:	outside
"I":	ownership

This structure might be allotted to Democritus, an early Greek philosopher who believed that there existed these indestructible tiny particles that compose all of what we call reality. Other Greek philosophers discussed the idea; if they accepted it, then they applied it to other areas of experience; and if they rejected it, then it dropped from their explanations of experience. Viewed more precisely (though certainly still over-simplified), the experiential structures might look like this:

Cognition:	atoms make up everything around us
Affect:	confidence
Behavior:	reflectively looking at tree
Sensation:	tree
Environ:	outside
"I":	ownership

which changes to:

Cognition:	image of tiny particles in conjunction with knowing that that is a tree
Affect:	increased confidence
Behavior:	more intensely reflectively looking at tree
Sensation:	less clear tree
Environ:	outside
"I":	ownership

which changes to:

Cognition:	that is grass
Affect:	slightly increased confidence
Behavior:	looking at grass
Sensation:	grass
Environ:	outside
"I":	ownership

which changes to:

Cognition:	image of tiny particles in conjunction with knowing that that is grass
Affect:	slightly increased confidence
Behavior:	looking at grass
Sensation:	grass
Environ:	outside
"I":	ownership

As we pass from one experience to another we do not get outside of the structure of experience. Let's say that the materialist's experiential structure looks something like the above. In positing that atoms make up all that is around us, he (let's say) is wholly within the structure of experience. The fact that he is claiming that there are such things as atoms that exist beyond what he is actually seeing exists, but only as a claim. That is, his claim in the first experience is that atoms make up everything around us. This claim is nothing other than an aspect of the cognitive component of the experience within which he participates. He is not looking at the atoms that supposedly make up the tree. Rather, he is looking at the tree itself. The experience within which he participates is constituted in part by the tree, but the tree in the first experience is being reflected upon. Therefore, it has a different quality than if it were not being reflected upon. For instance, if, just prior to reflecting upon the tree, the materialist were to look at the tree and appreciate its splendor, only to pass from this experience to the experience of asking a question in relation to the tree's constitution, and then to pass into the experience of claiming that the tree is constituted by atoms, then the set of experiences might look like this:

Cognition: beautiful tree
Affect: aesthetic feeling
Behavior: looking at tree
Sensation: tree
Environ: outside
"I":   ownership

which changes to:

Cognition: what is that tree ultimately made of?
Affect: curiosity
Behavior: looking reflectively at tree
Sensation: less than clear tree
Environ: outside
"I":   ownership

which changes to:

Cognition: atoms make up everything around us
Affect: confidence
Behavior: reflectively looking at tree
Sensation: tree
Environ: outside
"I":   ownership

- **Non-Reflective, Reflective, and Self-Reflective Experience**

The first experience in this set of experiences can be characterized as non-reflective. A *non-reflective experience* is an experience that is primarily characterized by the environmental component of experience. That is, the environmental component is focal in the experience; everything else is peripheral. So when the materialist is looking at the tree and feeling aesthetic beauty in relation to it, he is 'caught up' in the tree itself. Another type of non-reflective experience might be his looking at the tree like a botanist might look at it as he goes about classifying the tree. In other words, a non-reflective experience is an experience characterized by a focal environmental component.

When the materialist's experience shifts from "beautiful tree" to "what is the tree made of?", the focus shifts from the environment (tree) to the cognition (question). The tree, which was being felt aesthetically, is now replaced by the question regarding the tree's constitution. Simply because the materialist's experience shifts from focal environment to focal cognition does not mean that he has transcended the experiential structure. Rather, it means that because of *who he is in this situation*, his experiential structure shifts focus from the environmental to the cognitive component of experience. If the person were not a materialistic scientist or philosopher disposed to thinking of reality or being but, instead, an artist disposed to thinking of painting, then his experience might well shift from "beautiful tree" to "how can I capture this on canvas?" But since he is a materialistic scientist or philosopher, we will have him shift to "what is this tree ultimately made of?"

The point is, neither the person as materialist nor or as painter has transcended experience simply because his respective experiential structures have shifted focal components. The materialist participates in an experience focalized by the cognition, "what is this tree ultimately made of?", and the artist participates in an experience focalized by the cognition, "how can I capture this on canvas?" Each shift is a shift from non-reflective to reflective experience. *Reflective experience*, then, will be defined as those experiences consisting of cognition as the focal component.

But as the materialist is looking at the tree and experiencing its splendor, his friend asks him what he is doing? His experience now shifts to a *self-reflective experience* that could look like this:

Cognition: I'm looking at that beautiful tree
Affect: appreciation
Behavior: talking to friend
Sensation: friend
Environ: outside
"I":   ownership

Self-reflective experience refers to experiences in which the cognitive component consists of a *cognitivized "I"* and a *self-indicating component*. In this example, the cognitivized "I" is represented by the "I'm" in the cognition, and the self-indicating component is represented by the "looking" in the cognition. The "looking" refers to the behavioral component that points to or indicates him. The "tree" that refers to the actual tree in the environment is not a self-indicating component because it does not serve to point to or indicate the self, i.e. him.

The materialist has not gotten outside of the experiential structure within which he participates. There is no "I" or ego that transcends the cognition of "I'm looking at that beautiful tree". In this sense, experientialism concurs with existential phenomenology in its debunking of the transcendent ego, but it doesn't agree with its claim that the self-reflective experience consists of two parts: an ego and an object-of-consciousness. The existential phenomenologist might argue here that when the materialist reflects upon his looking at the tree, the mental aspect of his experience consists of his ego (self) and his looking-at-the-tree. But the experience as analyzed above does not have him looking at the tree at all. In fact, he is looking at his friend while he is saying that he is looking at the tree. Are we to hold the idea of "his-looking-at-the-tree" as the object of his ego or self, or are we to hold "his telling-his-friend-that-he-is-looking-at-the-tree" as the object of his ego? If the existential phenomenologist opts for the former, then he (let's say) gives cognition more ontological weight than the situation within which the person lives, and this idea tends to run contrary to Heidegger's argument for locating being (reality) within Dasein (being-in…a situation) (Heidegger, 1996). And if the existential phenomenologist opts for the latter, then he merges into Husserl's territory of a transcendent ego. It is the transcendental ego that is aware of the materialist's act of telling-his-friend-that-he-is-looking-at-the-tree. And Sartre has already rejected that notion.

- **Focal and Peripheral Consciousness**

Experientially consciousness is divided into focal and peripheral aspects. The focal aspect refers to that aspect of each component which dominates consciousness. The peripheral aspect refers to all the rest of the contents of consciousness. Peripheral contents vary in their intensity and impact upon the focal content, and all of them have the potential for entering focal consciousness. This can be represented in this fashion:

EXPERIENTIALISM

Focal Consciousness		Peripheral Consciousness
Cognition:	beautiful tree	orientation, realism of tree, knowledge of objects in environment, own body
Affect:	aesthetic feeling	confidence, comfortable, safe
Behavior:	looking at tree	standing, blinking, heart beating
Sensation:	tree	objects in environment, own body
Environ:	immediate outside	surrounding environment
"I":	ownership	ownership

Since the person in this example (we'll say) is in control of himself in this environment, the feeling of confidence is associated with orientation; since the person is familiar with the environment, the feeling of comfort is associated with knowledge of the environment. Both feelings of comfort and confidence support the knowledge of the realism of the tree. Safety is another feeling accompanying orientation in, and familiarity with, the environment. Any of these peripheral feelings could enter focal consciousness. For instance, if the person is asked a question in regard to his safety, he could easily assess his feeling of safety. When he does so, the aesthetic feeling will recede into peripheral consciousness.

The same dynamic could be applied to all contents within peripheral consciousness, even the realism of the tree which is located within the periphery of cognition, though this might well require other contents to enter peripheral consciousness before the realistic aspect of the cognitive periphery could change. For instance, if the person is taking a drug and is beginning to experience its effects, then the periphery of consciousness could be constituted in part by a fuzziness in visual sensation. As this fuzziness gets stronger and the sensation of the tree begins to alter from real to surreal, then the surreal peripheral content might overtake the real peripheral content and the tree will start to be seen as surreal. If the person cannot account through memory and reasoning for the introduction of the surreal aspect of the tree into the cognitive periphery, then he might experience some fear or curiosity in relation to this new content. As the surreal content becomes more pronounced, it could shift into focal consciousness. If the real content should never return to peripheral consciousness, then the person would have to adjust to the surreality of the tree.

Locating realism and surrealism in the peripheral aspect of the cognitive component of consciousness addresses the problem of realism that has plagued the mind:body problem throughout history. *How* we experience objects around us depends upon the contents of the cognitive component of experience in addition to the sensual components. The other components also exert an influence upon the realistic/surrealistic aspect of the cognitive periphery and the sensations. *That* we experience objects around us depends upon the environmental component of experience. Therefore, if we hallucinate a tree (a complete hallucination and not, let's say, a drug induced alteration of an actual tree), then a tree will not be the content of the environmental component of experience. In this case, we will have confused or conflated a type of surreal content of cognition with a real content, i.e. we will have understood the surreal content to be real. When we are able to differentiate surreal from real content, then we will have made significant movement toward understanding realism as an aspect of cognition without reducing objects in the environment to contents of the mind and without barring what has traditionally been referred to as the physical environment from being understood as-it-is, i.e. the total conditioning effect of the mind. Experientially, objects in the environment are contents of the environmental component of experience and not separate realities, independent of the "mind"; and the "mind" does not condition all of the objects in the environment (rationalism) because the "mind", experientially, is nothing other than the contents of the cognitive and/or affective components of experience, depending upon one's understanding of "mind".

- **The Cognitivized "I" and the Self-Indicating Component**

In the self-reflective experience, the cognitive component of consciousness consists of the cognitivized "I" of "I'm," the self-indicating component of "looking," and the rest of the cognition of "at that beautiful tree". Our Democritus has identified himself as the performer of the behavior of looking. The looking is *his* behavior. The behavior of looking points to or indicates him as the owner of the action. The tree does not coincide with his recognition of himself; rather, his behavior of looking does this. Hence, his behavior in this example is the self-indicating component of the cognitive component of experience. The rest of the cognition refers to what he is looking at. It connects a piece of history with the present moment. But nowhere is there any evidence of a splitting of the cognition into two separate components, i.e. ego and object-of-consciousness. The cognitivized "I," the self-indicating component, and the rest of the cognition are united into one cognition. And that cognition is owned [by Democritus].

When Hume sought to find the self through reflection, he could not find it as-it-is. Rather, he always "stumbled upon some particular perception or other, of heat or cold, light or shade, love or hatred, pain or pleasure. I never can catch *myself* at any time without a perception, and never can observe any thing but the perception" (Hume, 1988). When Russell sought to find the self, he noticed that "we always seemed to come upon some particular thought or feeling, and not upon the "I" which has the thought or feeling. Nevertheless there are some reasons for thinking that we are acquainted with the "I," though the acquaintance is hard to disentangle from other things" (Russell, 1988). Russell could not isolate the self from the thought or the feeling, but he knew that the self was not limited to the thought or the feeling; it was "something more" (my quotation).

The formula for phenomenology is: I – [awareness – object], where the "I" represents the ego, transcendent ego, or self, and the [awareness – object] represents that of which we are aware, whether that is a physical object in our environment or our own thoughts and feelings. In this view, there are two separate but interrelated 'entities': 1) the ego, self or "I" and 2) that of which the ego is aware. In this view, awareness (or consciousness) is like a medium that connects the "I" with the object.

But when we reflect upon ourselves, we will notice that every reflection involves one or more components of consciousness. Hume identified three pairs of sensations: heat:cold, light:shade, and pain:pleasure and one pair of feelings: love:hatred (Hume, 1969). Russell identified two of those components: cognition and affect (Russell, 1988). I wish to extend Russell's and Hume's list to include all components of consciousness. The following is a list of examples (with an analysis) of self-indicating components of consciousness:

Cognition: When asked what we are thinking about when we are engaged in multiplying, experience shifts from a reflective experience of multiplication to a self-reflective experience. The shift looks like this:

Cognition:	5 x 6 = 30
Affect:	interest
Behavior:	sitting reflectively
Sensation:	whatever we can sense in the room
Environ:	room
"I":	ownership

which changes to:

Cognition:	(what are you doing?)
Affect:	mild surprise
Behavior:	looking up at person
Sensation:	person
Eviron:	room
"I":	ownership

which changes to:

Cognition:	I'm multiplying
Affect:	slight pride
Behavior:	talking
Sensation:	other person
Environ:	room
"I":	ownership

The first experience in this set is a reflective experience. The "I" represents ownership of components of consciousness. The "I" is a function and not an ego, a self, an entity, a phenomenon or a thing. When we participate in a reflective experience, as we do in all experiences, we own the thought, feeling, behavior (both internal and external), sensation, and environment that constitute the experience. The thought (5x6=30) is *my* thought, the feeling (interest) is *my* feeling, etc.

This ownership is not to be confused with Husserl's transcendent ego. The transcendent ego is 'that' which is thinking a thought. The experiential "I" is not separate from the thought that constitutes the cognitive component of consciousness; it is co-existent with the thought. If the thought were to exist and not co-exist with ownership, then we would not know that we are thinking a thought. The thought might occur, but *we* would not be aware that we are thinking it. 'Thoughts' that might occur in sleep, while sleep-walking, while in a coma, while undergoing dissociation, or while in some similar altered state of consciousness might not be owned by us. Hence, they would not be real to us. If someone told us that we talked in our sleep, and we accept the idea that the behavior of talking is inextricably associated with cognition, and we have no experiential access to this event (e.g. a video-tape recording), then it is an event beyond our experience, and as such, not real to us. The report of it by the other person and all the ramifications of that report are certainly real to us though. The upshot of this is that if we do not own our own thoughts, then our cognition would be reduced to the function of a calculator or computer.

When the person in our example asks us what we are doing, our cognition shifts from 5x6=30 to our understanding the words that are being spoken by the person. Experience then shifts to "I'm multiplying". The "I'm" represents the cognitivized "I" and the "multiplying" represents the self-indicating component. To be a little more accurate, the "I" represents the cognitivized "I" and the "am" represents the tense in which the "I" exists. This tense will always be the present tense. Self-reflective experience is always constituted by the immediate present. Our reporting of what we are doing is an immediate present accounting of a past and present event. The self-indicating component of experience is our cognitive activity of thinking, i.e. multiplying. When we are simply multiplying, our multiplying exists without a cognitivized "I". We are "into" the multiplying. But when we are interrupted, our attention shifts from what we are thinking to reflection upon ourselves thinking. Some component or components of experience become focal in conjunction with a cognitivized "I". In this case, it is our thinking, or the cognitive component of consciousness, that connects us to ourselves. This cognitive component is referred to as a self-indicating component. It is what Russell identified when he reflected upon himself. What Russell couldn't name or grasp was the "something more" than a cognition. Experientialism refers to this something more as the function of ownership.

An experience that is constituted by a cognitivized "I" but is missing the function of ownership would be similar to those experiences reported by people who undergo depersonalized dissociative experiences. These people might know that an action is being performed but they are unsure as to whether or not they are performing it. They know that they are acting, but it doesn't seem like them doing the action. This idea is developed in *Emotional Investment: Transforming Psychotherapeutic Assumptions*. Suffice it to say right now that there are examples of experiences within which a cognitivized "I" might not be matched with the "I" as ownership.

Affect: When looking at some old photographs, we feel a sudden sadness. This set of experiences might look like this:

Cognition:	Here's one of Sandy on her rocking horse
Affect:	interest
Behavior:	looking at photograph
Sensation:	photograph
Environ:	room
"I":	ownership

which changes to:

Cognition:	I miss her so much
Affect:	sadness
Behavior:	staring at photograph
Sensation:	less clear photograph
Environ:	room
"I":	ownership

Here the first experience is non-reflective. The focus is on the photograph itself. The second experience replaces the first and now the focus is oneself feeling sad. The self-indicating component within this experience is the sadness. The person cognitivizes this sadness in terms of "miss her so much". She (let's say) behavioralizes this sadness in the activity of staring. But it is the sadness that points to her as owner of the cognitivized "I". She could also have thought something like: "(remembering her like) this makes me sad". Here she uses the term "sad" instead of "miss (her) so much".

Behavior: When a person dancing becomes aware that someone is looking at him (let's say) critically, the set of experiences might look like this:

Cognition: nice rhythm
Affect: happy
Behavior: dancing
Sensation: partner
Environ: dance floor
"I":   ownership
which changes to:
Cognition: she's looking at me critically
Affect: confusion
Behavior: dancing with puzzled look
Sensation: other person
Environ: dance floor
"I":   ownership
which changes to:
Cognition: I look stupid, don't I?
Affect: embarrassment
Behavior: slowed dancing, turning from other's gaze
Sensation: floor, people's legs, sick feeling in stomach
Environ: dance floor
"I":   ownership

    In this set of experiences it is the behavior of the individual that serves as the self-indicating component. He is not thinking that the critical gaze of the other is aimed at his hair, his clothes or anything else that might constitute the environmental component of experience. Rather, he is aware of his dancing. It is his behavior that is attached to the cognitivized "I" within the cognitive component of consciousness, and he owns the entire set of components.

Sensation: When a person is working on a puzzle at the kitchen table, he suddenly becomes aware of a hunger pang in his stomach. This set of experiences might look like this:

Cognition: where does this piece go?
Affect: slight irritation
Behavior: looking for place for piece
Sensation: puzzle

Environ: kitchen
"I":   ownership
which changes to:
Cognition: I'm hungry
Affect: interest (in food)
Behavior: looking absently at puzzle
Sensation: hunger pang
Environ: kitchen
"I":   ownership

In the second experience, it is the sensation of hunger that serves as the self-indicating component of the cognitive component of consciousness. The hunger is cognitivized as "hungry," but it could just as well have been cognitivized as "that food smells really good" (not in the context of an olfactory aesthetic analysis) or "I want something to eat". The sensation is behavioralized as "looking absently (staring briefly) at puzzle". The person isn't staring because he has lost interest in the puzzle. Rather, he is staring because the focus of his experience shifts from working the puzzle to realizing his hunger (sensation).

Environment: When a person wakes up and doesn't know where she is, the experiences might look like this:
Cognition: whose jacket is that?
Affect: curious
Behavior: looking at jacket
Sensation: jacket
Environ: room
"I":   ownership
which changes to:
Cognition: where am I?
Affect: fear
Behavior: glancing around room
Sensation: articles in room
Environ: room
"I":   ownership

In the second experience, it is not the fear that points to or indicates her as owner, but rather the room she is in. The room she is in is an inextricable part of the experience within which she participates, and it is that part of the experience that points to or indicates her. It is not a variety of stimuli composed of light and sound waves that causes her nervous system to respond in a particular fashion, which, in turn, activates her feeling of fear, causing her to look around the room. Such is a scientific analysis of the situation. Experientially, the scientific analysis is an explanatory accounting, and explanatory accountings are part-and-parcel experiential.

The "I": There is no example of the component of the "I" because the "I" is a function and not an isolatable component. The "I" as function can be cognized as in the cognitivized "I" (self-reflective experience), but it cannot be focalized as a separate entity. Like Hume and Russell, I cannot seem to isolate any 'I' or 'self' or 'ego' in self-reflective experience. It always seems to be attached to some component of consciousness. I can isolate that component and 'look' at it through my 'mental eye', but when I do this I am merely shifting into a reflective experience where the component itself becomes focal, all of which I own.

- **The Question of Relativism**

Equating reality with experience, when "experience" is defined as the necessary combination of components of consciousness as owned, opens the door for the development of a pure relativism. For if all experience is structured in this way, then how are we to tell which experiences are 'right' and which are 'wrong' when we are faced with contradictory claims? After all, the theist claims that God exists independently of human beings, and the atheist claims that God doesn't exist at all and that he is a product of human imagination. So is the theist or the atheist right? Or are they both wrong? It seems that they can't both be right, unless we accept the relativist thesis that all people's realities are right, even if they contradict each other. Does experientialism side with the relativists? If we cannot get outside of experience to any supposed objective reality, then how do we deal with conflicting experiential realities?

For experientialism, traditionally conceived objective reality as reality with a nature of its own apart from human experience must be transformed into the objective reality of experience itself. After Descartes re-located the objective reality of the supernatural from heaven to the natural mind and made the mind the ultimate determiner of reality, he then proceeded to explore the ideas in the mind (at least his mind) so he could elaborate on what constitutes reality. There he found the ideas of God-as-objective-reality and nature-as-objective-reality, among various other ideas. When Kant re-located all supernatural and natural objective realities within the human mind and did not allow them to get back outside of the mind, as Descartes had done, he proceeded to explore the 'real' objective reality, i.e. the structure of the mind. All things supernatural and natural were eliminated from objective reality. They were inaccessible. When experientialism re-locates traditionally conceived objective realities within experience, it forces 'objective reality' to transform itself not into ideas in the mind (Descartes) or into the structure of the mind (Kant) or into matter existing outside and constitutive of the mind (material empiricism) but into the structure of experience itself.

Experience consists of six components. All of these components must exist for there to be experience. And all of these components support each other and sustain each other's existence. So when a conflict arises between people who are making opposing objective claims, it is not *that* which corresponds with the claim that is objective reality, but rather it is *how* that claim is made that constitutes objective reality. It is not that there actually is a God who created the world that is ontologically relevant; rather, it is that this belief or claim constitutes the cognitive component of a simple, strong and right experiential structure that is ontologically relevant. The same holds true for the idea that we are the product of billions of years of changing matter. Since neither the creationist nor the evolutionist can get outside of the experiential structures within which they participate, any claims they make in relation to objective realty-beyond-experience are of absolutely no consequence to anyone. What is of great consequence, though, is the fact that they are making, believing in, and acting upon the claim.

If objective reality is relocated within experience, thus making claims relative to each other, and if pure relativism is something difficult, if not impossible, to maintain, then how are we to deal with conflicting objective claims? Let's look at the structures of two conflicting experiences to answer this question:

Cognition:	that object is red	Cognition:	that object is dark gray
Affect:	confidence	Affect:	confidence
Behavior:	looking at object	Behavior:	looking at object,
	talking		talking
Sensation:	object	Sensation:	object
Environ:	object in room	Environ:	object in room
"I":	ownership	"I":	ownership

- **Simple, Strong and Right (SSR) Experiences:**
  Let's say that both of these experiences are structurally simple, strong, and right (SSR). Negatively put, by *simple* I mean that the structure of the experience is not complex. Complex experiences will be made clear in the next section on "Compound and Complex Experiences."

  "Simple" might also be understood, though less accurately, as focal components of experience that are singular and consistent, i.e. there is only one content for each component. This means that the components consist of one focal content and a number of subordinate peripheral contents. For instance, in the first experience, the cognition "that object is red" consists of the focal content of the idea "that object is red", whereas the peripheral contents of the cognitive component are numerous and include: knowing where I am, knowing where the object is in relation to other objects, knowing what some or all of the other objects are, knowing that I have a slight ache in my head, knowing that I am standing and looking at the object, knowing that the object is an object and not a part of that upon which the objects rests, knowing that the object is a solid, three-dimensional object and not a hologram or a hallucination, etc.

  The cognition is accompanied by the affect of confidence. The cognition does not cause the affect, as some sciences or cognitive psychology might maintain. Rather, it co-exists with the affect and the affect supports the existence of the cognition. This means that if the affect were to change, then the cognition would also change, to one that was consistent with the new affect. The affective component is also focally singular and any other peripheral feelings are subordinate to the focal content. For instance, the focal affect of "confidence" might be accompanied by any number of peripheral contents which include: a feeling of curiosity as to why I am doing what I'm doing, a slight feeling of irritation because I don't like being in situations where I don't know exactly what I'm doing, a residual feeling of the embarrassment I felt when I volunteered for this demonstration, an overall feeling of belonging in this room with these people, etc.

The cognition and the affect co-exist with the behavioral component, which is divided into "interior" and "exterior" aspects. The interior aspect refers to the physiology of my body, and the exterior aspect refers to my body's comportment in relation to my environment. Focally, I am looking at the object in a particular way, so as to describe its color. Peripherally, I am in the standing comportment, I am moving my eyes in a certain way; my heart is beating at a certain pace, etc.

The cognition, affect, and behavior are accompanied by a set of sensations. Focally, I see the object. Peripherally, I see the desk upon which the object rests, I see parts of the room, I hear myself talking, I feel a slight pang of hunger, I feel a slight ache in my foot, I smell the odor in the room, I taste the roof of my mouth as my tongue rubs against it, etc.

These four components of consciousness are joined by the environmental component. The focal aspect of this component is the object that I am looking at. The peripheral aspect includes: the room, some objects in the room, the light and sounds in the room, the odors in the room, parts of outside of the room, etc. The peripheral aspects of the environmental component will tend to mirror the peripheral aspects of the sensational and cognitive components that correspond with the sensational components. For instance, though I am focused on the object while being in a room, the aspects of the room that are in the periphery of my sensual field are also in the periphery of the environmental component of consciousness. The environment is restricted to the focal:peripheral content of the components that make up the experience within which I participate. The environment is inextricably *attached* to the other components of consciousness.

When the content of the focal components of consciousness is singular and the peripheral contents are subordinate to the focal content, then the experiential structure is said to be simple.

Experiential structures can also be simple and complicated. *Complicated experiences* are simple experiences that consist of layers of componential content, e.g. when one splits one's focus and is focally aware of two things at virtually the same time. An example of this would be driving a car while thinking of something other than driving. Both the driving (road, etc.) and that which one is thinking about share focal consciousness, one perhaps more prominent than the other at any given time. Such experiences can be represented as a serial structure, where one simple experience replaces the other in time, or as a complicated structure, where one vacillates with the other in focal consciousness.

An experience is *strong* when it tends to produce *confirmation experiences*. A confirmation experience is an experience, experiential structure, or frame (synonyms) that confirms the rightness of the *initial* or *target experience* (i.e. the experience being analyzed). For instance, I might look at the object again when I hear that the other person identified the color of the object as dark gray. The second look serves as a confirmation experience in relation to the first look. I experience it again as red. Another example of a confirmation experience is the creationist's experience of the Bible passage and the evolutionist's citing various facts in various sciences. These experiences confirm the rightness of their respective target experiences. Confirmation experiences do not confirm "what" is being held to be real. Rather, they confirm the rightness of the target experience's structure.

The *rightness* of an experience refers to the contents of the structure in support of the identity of the person. It is "who I am in this situation." For example, the person identifying the object as red is who this person is in this situation, i.e. me seeing object as red. If I were to be given a drug that alters my perception, and I see the object as dark gray, and I am not aware, either focally or peripherally, that my perception has been influenced by a drug, then who I am in this situation is a person who sees the object as dark gray. But it is likely that, if given a drug to alter my perception, the perception will not be exactly the same as it would have been if I had perceived a gray object. Hence, it might be very difficult, if not impossible, for me to see the same dark gray while on the drug then I would have seen if not on the drug. But if the difference in perceptions is so slight, then it could be rendered insignificant. And if insignificant, then I could be said to be "who I am in this situation," i.e. me seeing the object as dark gray.

If both experiences above are simple, strong and right, then that which is being claimed in each experience is real. The object *is* red for the person who sees it as red, and the object *is* dark gray for the person who sees it as dark gray. And neither person can get outside of the structures within which he (let's say) participates to prove to the other that what he maintains to be the case is the case. Experientially, any notion of 'is the case' or 'is not the case' is opening the door for meta-experiential construction.

Science might respond by arguing that the light wave frequencies that enter both people's eyes are the same, regardless of how they might be experienced by the people. Therefore, the light waves are objective realities, independent of anyone's experience. Experientially, the scientist's assertion that the light waves' frequencies are the same is based on his (let's say) indirect observations of such, and these observations are nothing other than sensational components of consciousness. These components inextricably co-exist with the other components of consciousness, as owned. As sensual observations, then, the scientific response would be grounded in experience. And as rational inference, the scientific response would be solidly grounded in the cognitive component of consciousness. But when science moves beyond this and draws the conclusion that these light wave frequencies exist beyond experience without owning the conclusion, it has created a meta-experiential construct that has no basis in experience.

Even if light wave frequencies could be directly observed as environmental phenomena, they could only be observed in conjunction with cognition (and the other components of consciousness). Any environment ontologically separated from cognition is a distortion of reality.

A similar criticism can be leveled against supernatural realism. Supernatural realism maintains that certain 'things' or 'beings' exist and have a nature of their own, whether any human being is around to experience them or not. But when the experiential structure of any supernatural claim is analyzed, it is found that the reality of the thing or being that is claimed is absolutely nowhere to be found. For instance, when a theist claims that:

Cognition: God exists
Affect: confidence

Behavior:	talking
Sensation:	other person
Environ:	other person, room
"I":	ownership

she (let's say) is making a traditional objective claim, but the claim's objectivity lies not in the fact that her claim matches any 'greater reality' that exists beyond the experience within which she participates. It lies, rather, in the structure of experience itself. If the experience is simple, strong and right, then the claim is real. And simply because the claim is real does not mean that it matches any 'greater reality'. Whether it matches a greater reality or not is inconsequential. That which might exist beyond experience is of no use to us. Until it becomes a part of someone's experience, it is virtually non-existent.

Let's take a hypothetical example to make this clearer. A woman develops some aches and pains that she doesn't recognize (i.e. cannot identify or label). These are new experiences for her. She goes to a doctor and the doctor listens to her words and observes her behavior and is not sure what to make of it. The list of symptoms doesn't seem to fit any diagnostic criteria for any known disease, so he consults with another doctor. They decide it might be Y-disease that is afflicting her, and they prescribe medication-P. The medication fails to alter the woman's symptoms.

If we stop our example here and ask, what is real in this situation, we come up with a list that includes: the woman's aches and pains, the doctor's understanding of her aches and pains, the doctor's confusion, the doctor's decision, the prescribed medicine, the woman having taken the medication, and the continuation of the aches and pains. Though oversimplified, we could stop here and say that this is all that is real. *That* which is causing the woman's aches and pains is unknown altogether. That is, there is no thought, idea, image, understanding or cognition of any sort that is attached to an environmental component that is the cause of the woman's symptoms. The doctor might hypothesize that it is a bacterium that is causing her symptoms, but what is real here is:

Cognition:	I believe that a type of bacterium is causing these symptoms
Affect:	doubtful confidence

Behavior:	talking
Sensation:	patient
Environ:	room
"I":	ownership

Clearly, we can see here that there exists no actual bacterium within the doctor's experiential structure. The "word" bacterium is certainly a constituent of the experience. The thought, "bacterium", is a part of the structure, but the environmental component of the experience does not contain a bacterium, either focally or peripherally.

The material empiricist might object and say that the bacterium would exist within the patient's environmental component, not the doctor's. So let's analyze the patient's experiential structure and see. Her structure might look like this:

Cognition:	I believe I have a bacterium in me causing this pain
Affect:	doubtful confidence
Behavior:	talking (to another person), rubbing belly
Sensation:	other person, belly, aches and pains
Environ	room, belly
"I":	ownership

Again, there doesn't seem to be any bacterium in experience. To be sure there is the doubtful belief that a bacterium is causing the aches and pains, and certainly the aches and pains are real, but beyond this she cannot go. Until that bacterium (if it is a bacterium that is causing the aches and pains) enters an experiential structure within which someone is participating, then the existence of it is wholly inconsequential. Even if the doctors discover a new bacterium, study it, and develop a drug to combat it, the existence of the bacterium-beyond-experience is inconsequential. But the existence of the bacterium-within-experience is very consequential. The hypothesis that it exists can prompt a set of experiences that can lead to a discovery of a new bacterium and eventually to a cure for the disease.

Again, the material empiricist (scientist) might object. He might contend that the doctor who discovers the bacterium is finding it in the woman or at least outside of his own mind. Clearly, his own mind is not conditioning the existence of the bacterium, as Kant might contend, and, hence, his own experience is not dictating the existence of the bacterium. In fact, the reverse is the case: the actual bacterium is determining the existence of his sensations and the thoughts connected to them.

This argument, and all materialistic empirical arguments, rests upon a distorted dualistic ontology. Simply because the doctor experiences the bacterium to exist independently of his own mind does not mean that he has broken free of experience and discovered the bacterium as-it-is, apart from human experience. If we were to analyze this experience, it might look like this:

Cognition: a new thing
Affect: excited
Behavior: looking through microscope
Sensation: thing
Environ: lab
"I":   ownership

At this point the doctor is aware that the 'thing' he is looking at is a thing rather than an aspect of another thing, etc. But up to this point, what the thing is, other than its being a thing, is unknown. If we look beyond the focal cognition of "a new thing" and into the periphery of the cognitive component of consciousness, we find the content of "thing-ness" or "object-ness". That is, the doctor could have cognized the thing not as a thing, separate from other things, but as an extension of another thing, e.g. an anomaly or a deformity. But he did not. And we cannot at this point contend that he did not understand it to be an extension of another thing because it, 'in fact', is not an extension but a thing itself, because the experience within which such an understanding exists does not yet exist! That experience in which the doctor *contends* that the thing he is looking at is a thing, separate from other things, does not yet exist. What exists at this point is the understanding that the thing he is looking at is a thing, separate from other things. This pair of experiences could look like this:

	Focal	**Peripheral**
Cognition:	realism of 'thing'	understanding of other things, apart from the new thing, understanding of looking into a microscope, understanding of being in a

room, etc.

Affect:	excited	
Behavior:	looking through microscope	
Sensation:	thing	
Environ:	thing in lab	
"I":	ownership	

which changes to:

Cognition:	I understand this thing to be a thing because it is in fact a thing	image of thing
Affect:	confident	
Behavior:	sitting, reflecting	
Sensation:	environment	
environ:	room	
"I":	ownership	

The first experience contains the content of "thing-ness" in the periphery of the cognitive component of consciousness. The second experience does not contain "thing-ness" in the periphery of consciousness. It doesn't even contain the thing as a component of the environment. Rather, it contains, at best, an image of the thing. The thing-ness of the thing has become the subject of the doctor's thinking. The thing-ness of the thing has become the focal aspect of the explanatory experience within which the doctor participates. When he assumes that the explanatory experience is somehow more real than the experience within which the understanding of thing-ness exists in relation to looking at the thing, then he is creating a meta-experiential construct, i.e. a distortion of reality. Instead of understanding the explanation he gives in conjunction to his initial experience as a confirmation experience of the rightness of his initial experience, he awards the explanatory experience ontological primacy over that of the initial experience.

What the doctor has done is to focalize a peripheral component of his experience of looking at the thing and made that peripheral component the reason why he experiences the thing as a thing. This is a fundamental distortion of reality.

- **Compound and Complex Experiences**

A compound experience refers to any two or more simple, strong and right (SSR) experiences that conflict with each other. When the creationist is first exposed to the theory of evolution, she (let's say) may experience a conflict. She is invested in her belief in creationism (i.e. it is who she is), but she is interested in the theory of evolution (partially invested). The interest might vacillate with repulsion, but if the interest experience is stronger than the repulsion experience, then it will prompt more confirmation experiences, and the interest in the theory will grow. She will start thinking more about evolution, working through some of the conceptual problems, and these experiences will be countered by confirmation experiences in relation to her belief in creationism. If the evolutionist experiences are stronger than the creationist experiences, then the person will change her beliefs. She will reject the creationist stance and adopt the evolutionist stance.

Compound experiences are an unavoidable part of life and an integral part of change and growth. They can arise from individual experiential processes or, more usually, from interpersonal experiential processes.

Complex experiences refer to experiential structures that have become skewed or distorting of reality. The creation of complex experiential structures is often the product of interpersonal dynamics. Complex structures do not usually arise from individual experience.

For example, if the creationist's interest in evolution were real (SSR), but she was not able to express her interest (live it) around other people for fear of their rejection, then she would engage in complex experiential construction. She would split herself into two selves, the one who is interested in evolution and seeks out more on the subject, and the one who doesn't want to incur the rejection of others who are important to her. Her evolutionist self is clandestine in relation to her creationist self.

But if her evolutionist experiences are stronger than her creationist experiences, then her weaker experience is the one she shows to those who are important to her, and her stronger experience is the one she engages in secret. The experience is complex. The stronger experience has gone 'underground' and the weaker experience is shown to others. If the weaker experience is honed to appear sincere, then she might well gain the acceptance, if not the accolades, of others, but such acceptance is ultimately hollow. A false self is created. And if the person comes to 'live in' the false self, and profess a belief in it (i.e. defend it), then the complex structure is complete. The false self has become more real than the real self (SSR experiences). A complex structure can be represented in this fashion:

	Real Self	False Self
Cognition:	[I believe in evolution]*	I believe in creationism
Affect:	[confidence}	pseudo-confidence
Behavior:	[expressing belief]	false-witnessing
Sensation:	[other person]	other "person" **
Environ:	[person in room]	"person" in room
"I":	ownership	

* The brackets represent the stronger of two experiences that has been denied, repressed, suppressed, or overridden by the weaker experience.

** "person" is in quotations because that aspect of the person has become more an object to be confronted than a person to be respected.

Rousseau captured the complex structure in his political philosophy when he said that "The strongest is never strong enough to be master all the time, unless he transforms force into right and obedience into duty" (Rousseau, 1987). Applied to our example, those who are important to the woman are in the position of master. They have power over her. Their rejection of her can cause her great pain, if not perceived psychological destruction or self destruction. They represent the "stronger" in this situation. They are stronger because they transformed force into right and obedience into duty. They do not use the threat of physical force to make the woman obey their will; rather, they convert physical force into psychological force and, instead, threaten the psychological life of the woman. And if they are successful in their efforts, they and the woman will convince themselves that they have the right to impose their will upon her and that she has the duty to obey them.

Complex structures can be plotted along a continuum. At one end of the continuum, the experiential structures that constitute the complex experience are clearly in conflict, and the person knows he (let's say) is misrepresenting himself or deceiving others. At the other end of the continuum, the structures are nearly isomorphic, and the person doesn't know he is deceiving himself or others; he 'believes' in what he does. But this isomorphism is never really complete. It is falseness passing for truth. Rousseau's strong masters fall into this category; they have convinced themselves that they have a right to impose their will on others; and others have convinced themselves that they have a duty to obey.

- **Immediate and Explanatory Experiences**

Immediate experience refers to all experiential structures. It is the experience occurring *now*. *Explanatory experience* refers to a particular type of immediate experience, one that refers to, and affirms the rightness of, an immediate experience.

For example, at some point in an evolutionist's life, he (let's say) conceives the idea that we as a species have evolved over millions of years. When he conceives this idea, he is not himself traversing those millions of years. Hence, all aspects of those millions of years are not constituents of any experience within which he participates. Rather, the *idea* is a part of experience. The idea constitutes the cognitive component of the experiential structure within which he participates. As such, it is part of an immediate experience. But this experience is not just an immediate experience. It is also an explanatory experience. It explains how we human beings have come to inhabit this world. Up to this point, the evolutionist is on good experiential ground. He is offering an explanation of the origin of human beings (and possibly the entire universe). But then there takes place an ontological slight of mind. The evolutionist *disowns* his own cognition. He *extracts* himself from experience and offers an explanation of all experience without recognizing that his explanation is just another immediate experience, though a different type from the others.

The most an explanatory experience can do is to confirm the rightness of another immediate experience. In conceiving that we have evolved over millions of years, the evolutionist confirms the rightness of all those related experiences which preceded the confident proclamation.

Let's say that the evolutionist had been raised a creationist. He was taught at home and throughout grade school that God created the world. And he accepted this idea without much question. But when he attended high school, he was introduced to the theory of evolution. His experiences of creation and evolution conflicted with each other. At first, he resisted accepting evolution as a better theory than creationism, but he was strongly attracted to the theory of evolution nevertheless. The more he investigated the theory, the greater his appreciation and acceptance of it, and the more he rejected the legitimacy of creationism. All of the experiences in which he participated that served to prompt the target experience above can be thought of as confirmation experiences. All of the experiences which follow in the wake of the target experience that are consistent with the target experience are also confirmation experiences. So confirmation experiences, as a descriptor, can be applied to experiences that come before or after the target experience as long as they are consistent with the target experience. The target experience can also be a confirmation experience of some other target experience. The sum total of confirmation experiences in regard to a particular intellectual issue composes the theory of that issue. A theory is a set of inter-related confirmation experiences that address a certain issue or issues in a consistent manner.

- **Theory Building**

Foucault argues that knowledge in the sciences is not simply facts in conjunction with theories that explain facts, but it is also "a space in which the subject may take up a position…, a field of coordination and subordination of statements in which concepts appear…, and is defined by the possibilities of use and appropriation offered by discourse…." (Foucault, 1972). He understands scientific knowledge to be a collection of situations and lived experiences which have become 'distilled' into theories and scientific laws.

Much like Heidegger who argues that science is an enterprise that systematically reduces being-in-the-world (Da-Sein) to a 'construction' of being (Heidegger, 1996), Foucault argues that the various scientific discourses are the products of their respective historical situations. Neither Heidegger nor Foucault could accept the materialistic empirical 'objectivies' of science. They understand science to be inextricably enmeshed in lived human experience.

Earlier, James and the pragmatists framed the sciences within collections of material and immaterial observations, ideas, and theories that are coherent in their own right. For James, reality was less the objective world outside of human experience and more a coherent collection of subjective (mental) and objective (physical) 'worlds' (James, 1981).

Experientialism, likewise, maintains that the sciences are not the products of objective or quasi-objective fact gathering based on observation in conjunction with explanatory theories but rather compilations of interconnected experiences that serve to confirm (or disconfirm) each other. Materialistic science, as a method of knowing, distorts reality by reducing it to the physical environment. It bases its construction of reality upon the assumption that all reality is physical in nature. Idealistic science (ala Berkeley), as a method of knowing, also distorts reality by reducing it to cognition (although Berkeley argues for a supernatural rather than a natural origin of knowledge). Materialistic science uses the senses to 'get to' the material world and tries to develop its theories based on sensual information. It uses cognition to manipulate the sensual content so as to unify the various and sundry sense data, but it tends not to recognize that it is doing so. Rather, it 'bypasses' or 'forgets' this characteristic of "being-in-the-world" and assumes that observations are devoid of the other components of consciousness, especially that of affect, and scientific theories present themselves as rational, detached, unemotional determinations of reality.

The experientialist argument against materialistic science is simple once its ontological framework is accepted. Science reduces reality to one component of experience and seeks to explain all the other components of reality in terms of that one component. Hence, it takes reality, which is manifold, and reduces it to matter, seeking to explain the manifold in terms of matter. But each explanation is nothing other than more experiences either confirming or disconfirming other experiences.

The real power of materialistic science lies in the SSR structures of explanatory experience. The false power of materialistic science lies in its ability to convert force into right and obedience into duty. Force, in this case, is ideological. Scientists do not normally physically force someone to do their will. This tends to be against the law. They are not supposed to trick anyone into doing their will either. But scientists can exert their power over others by establishing their version of reality as reality-beyond-experience. Scientists can convince themselves that they have the right to impose their beliefs upon others inasmuch as they believe that they have captured reality-beyond-experience, and that others have the duty to obey them, for their own good.

Hence, psychiatrists can commit patients against their will into mental hospitals for their own good; medical boards can deny licensure to people against their own will for the good of the public; therapists can convince clients that they have a disorder when clients resist such a notion; studies can create the illusion of objectivity and statistical analyses can fortify that illusion.

- **The Self**

When Descartes moved the locus for determining reality from God's heaven, the Bible, and the clergy to the human mind, he set the stage for the naturalization of the self. In Descartes' system, the self lies between the physical world of objects and the spiritual world of God, as it does for Augustine and Aquinas, but Kant's hermetically sealed rationalism argued away the objective existence of nature and forced a division of the rationalist world into the transcendent ego (self) and everything else mental. The physical world as-it-is was unreachable; only our version of the physical world was attainable. But Kant was not primarily a relativist. He objectified the reality of reason, the categories of mind (e.g. space, time, causation, etc.), and other things mental. For Kant, the structure of mind was objective reality.

So within Kant's rationalism, when we look at a physical object in the environment, we see a particular object, as opposed to other objects, and/or as opposed to the background or environment within which the object is located, but this object is an object not because it possesses qualities of 'object-ness' outside of our minds, but rather because our minds dispose us to experience the object as an object.

For instance, if we look at an object (e.g. a cup) on another object (e.g. a desk) in a room, we know that the object is *an* object, separate from other objects like the desk, because our minds automatically confer the notion of 'object-ness' to the object. We could have looked at the cup and understood it as just a part of the desk which projected out and had a different color and texture, etc. In other words, the cup would not be an object in itself but part of an object. The same could be said about the desk and the floor it rests upon. The fact that human beings can see objects as objects is, for Kant, the result of innate categories of mind.

So in Kant's rationalistic system, if we are to study reality, we need to study the structure of our own minds and see how our minds condition all that we come into contact with, even our own bodies. But how do we study the structure of our own minds? What constitutes the "we" in that question?

In order to study the structure of the mind and its effects upon the world around us, Kant had to utilize the notion of a transcendent ego. The transcendent ego is that which studies the structure of the mind and its effect on the environment. The transcendent ego is at once 'in' the mind and 'apart' from it. It is at once similar to and dissimilar from the rest of the mind. And since the categories of mind were, for Kant, objective realities, then it was natural for him to think that the transcendent ego was also an objective reality.

Kant and the medieval thinkers had one thing in common: their idea of the self was primarily a static one. Though the Catholic Church established the age of reason to be about seven years, and hence, allotted some thought to developmental ideas, the self or soul was something given to us whole by God and not subject to development. We could put stains on our souls when we sinned, but that was the only way the soul was subject to change. Kant eliminated the changeability of the soul or self (transcendent ego) altogether. For Kant, it was like we human beings were born adults. He was not very concerned about development.

It was Hegel who introduced the notion of change into ontological constructions. This change in philosophy paralleled a growing recognition in the young sciences of the importance of the scientific method. Science recognized that the physical world outside of the human mind, which included the human body, needed to be understood as much as possible on its own terms, i.e. as it really is and not just as we understand it to be. But at the same time, science realized that scientists were people, subject to human limitations, and, hence, had to understand this world through the mind. Since the mind can distort the physical world, it was important to keep grounding statements, theories, and laws about physical reality *in* physical reality. In order to keep our biases and distortions to a minimum, scientists had to support their claims with empirical evidence. The more evidence there was, the stronger the claim.

But this method of determining reality admitted of a continuous process of grounding and re-grounding understanding in the empirical world. Not only were people set up by Descartes and Kant to be the ultimate determiners of reality, but now the history of people was introduced into ontological determinations. What people determine to be real at one time might not align with what they determine to be real at a later time. Change is inherent within the scientific method. And change is inherent within Hegel's dialectical ontological system. Hegel accepted Kant's rationalism, admitting that the mind conditions everything it comes into contact with, but he rejected Kant's hermetically sealed version of rationalism. Hegel accepted science's empirical leanings, along with its underlying realism, but he rejected its hermetically sealed version of it, i.e. materialism. For Hegel (at least one aspect of Hegel), reality was determined by the interaction between the human mind and the physical world. The mind acted upon the environment as it understood it to be, and the environment "acted" upon the human mind as it did. If human understanding of the environment did not match the environment's action upon the mind, then the mind either had to re-organize itself in relation to the environment or find ways to alter the environment to fit its understanding of it. When the mind re-organized itself, it changed. When it changed, so too did our understanding of the environment.

Where Hegel parted with science was in his contention that this dynamic interplay between mind and physical world was transpiring within a grander objective idealism. Hegel invited religious supernaturalism back into his naturalistic accounting of reality by arguing that the dialectic between mind and body, the mental and the physical, the many and the one took place within an objective ideality of spirit. Spirit was the all-embracing reality that was evolving through the dialectic between mind and body. So even though Hegel rejected Kant's hermetically sealed version of rationalism by allowing a real mind to interact with a real physical world, thus producing reality, he affirmed the mind or the mental as objective. The physical world was subject to or dependent upon the evolution of the mind.

Balancing Hegel's dialectical idealism was Marx's dialectical materialism. Marx accepted the dialectic between the mind and the body (matter), but he rejected the all-embracing ideality of spirit. Instead, he located the objective, all-embracing aspect of reality in economic organization (Marx, 1988). It is how we organize ourselves economically that gives rise to and conditions other ontology-producing activities, i.e. religion, science, government, etc. In grounding ultimate reality in economic organization, Marx aligned himself with the material realism that underlay the methods of science. In grounding ultimate reality in spirit, Hegel aligned himself with the idealism that underlay religion. The battle between mind and body, the mental and the physical, the many and the one continued.

For Hegel, the self is an active agent that interacts with and alters its environment, and that environment, in turn, interacts with and alters that self. The dialogue between self and environment takes place in time, and the self is continually changing itself into something new. The self is dynamic. For Marx, the self is the result of economic forces. The proletariat's self differs from the bourgeois self in that the proletariat finds meaning for being within the determinations of the bourgeoisie. One class of people creates a self for another class of people by exploiting them economically. Marx agreed with Rousseau when he said that a master is as much a slave as the slave, because in order to retain his position of power the master must be ever vigilant in his control of the slave, thus giving the slave power over him. But ultimately, when push comes to shove, it is better to be a master than a slave. The freedom and the spoils are to the master's advantage.

Hegel's sense of self aligned quite well with traditional religion and Kantian rationalism, and Marx's sense of self aligned quite well with materialistic empiricism. Again, we see the mind:matter or mind:body problem at work.

Husserl picked up where Hegel left off when he posited his theory of intentionality. When Husserl said that whenever we are conscious, we are necessarily conscious of something (i.e. his theory of intentionality), he linked consciousness with an object of consciousness (Husserl, 1931). The idea that consciousness is something totally separate from those things of which we are conscious was rejected. The empirical conception of reality that preceded Husserl's phenomenological conception argued that the world outside of the mind (and consciousness) existed 'on its own' and that the world inside of the mind (consciousness) likewise existed 'on its own'. That is, the empiricist accepted both the rationalistic idea that we cannot get outside of our minds so as to understand the world around us as it is and, hence, are subject continuously to conditioning that outside world, and the realistic idea that there is, in fact, a world outside of our minds that has a nature of its own, whether we are in contact with it or not. But Husserl argued that the conception of 'two worlds' (mind and matter, mental and physical, etc.) was faulty because we can never be simply conscious. Whenever we are conscious, we must be conscious of something, whether that something is mental (e.g. thoughts, feelings) or physical (e.g. tables, behavior). The theory of intentionality forces a necessary link between mind (consciousness) and mind (thoughts, feelings) or between mind (consciousness) and body or matter (physical environment, including our own body). If we understand Husserl's theory of intentionality to be the first step in integrating the mind with the environment (or the world outside of the mind), and the first step in defining consciousness as something more than a medium or state of being through which we know the world, then we might be in a better position to understand and appreciate the fundamental shift in thinking that an experientialist conception of reality and ethics might afford.

Let's take Husserl's lead and transform it. If we understand the mind's connection to the world outside of the mind to be represented linearly as: "I"–consciousness–object, then Husserl's theory of intentionality alters this fundamental representation to look like this: "I"–[consciousness–object]. Consciousness cannot be understood without an object of consciousness.

If we flesh out the objects of consciousness imbedded within the theory of intentionality and identify all of the possible objects of consciousness, it seems that we will find:

EXPERIENTIALISM

- Cognition: which includes all thoughts, ideas, understandings, images, memories, etc. that are 'in our minds'
- Affect: which includes all emotions, feelings, and moods
- Behavior: which includes internal behaviors or aspects of physiology and external behaviors or comportment
- Sensation: which includes sensations and sense data from all senses
- Environment: which includes all aspects of the physical world outside of our minds (including our own bodies) with which we are in contact

When we are conscious, we are necessarily conscious of something. That "something," I am arguing, consists of all of the components listed above. This contention can be verified experientially by answering the following question: When you are conscious, what are you conscious of? Possible answers are: objects in the environment (in motion or standing still), light, sounds, thoughts, feelings, memories, relationships, moods, own body, looking, moving, people (in motion or standing still), odors, crying, etc. These 'objects' can be categorized in this fashion:

Cognition:	Affect:	Behavior:	Sensation:	Environment:
thoughts	feelings	moving	light	objects
relationships	moods	crying	sounds	own body
memories	emotions	looking	odors	people

When you reflect upon yourself, what exactly constitutes your reflection, or what is it that you are reflecting upon? Possible answers: face, body, blemishes, clothes, odors, aspirations, wanting, traits, aches, happiness, irritable, rocking, blinking, anger, bleeding, tickles, hunger, crying, tapping fingers, scratching head, memories, goals, pressure in stomach, things to do, being conscious, boredom, clothes, itches, proximity to others, relation to room, interest, memories, etc. These objects of self-reflection can be categorized in this fashion:

Cognition:	Affect:	Behavior:	Sensation:	Environment:
aspirations	wanting	rocking	aches	face
traits	happiness	blinking	tickles	body

memories	irritable	tapping	itches	blemishes
goals	boredom	scratching	hunger	proximity to others
things to do	anger	bleeding	odors	relation to room
being conscious	interest	crying	pressure in stomach	clothes

When Husserl's theory of intentionality is fleshed out, we can see that when we are conscious, we are conscious of components of consciousness, and when we are conscious of ourselves (self-reflection), we are also conscious of components of consciousness. The difference between consciousness and experience is the owning of components of consciousness. In experience, these are *my* thoughts, *my* feelings, *my* behaviors, *my* sensations, and *my* environment. The "I", or ownership, is inextricably intertwined in the structure of experience. And experience is ontological.

The traditional triad: "I" – consciousness – object and Husserl's significant alteration of it into the dualistic "I" – [consciousness – object] is altered yet again into the "monistic" experiential structure. Experientially, not only does the object of consciousness collapse into consciousness itself, but so too does the "I". We cannot detach the ownership of components of experience from those components without destroying experience altogether.

In a non-reflective experience, we are not focally aware of ourselves, but we *are* peripherally aware of ourselves. For instance, when we are listening to a piece of music, we might be caught up in the music and not be aware of ourselves listening to it. The experience might look like this:

Cognition: solo violin
Affect: longing
Behavior: listening
Sensation: violin sound
Environ: violin sound in room
"I":   ownership

In this experience we own our knowledge of what instrument is making the sound we are listening to; we own the longing we feel in relation to the sound; we own the listening behavior in which we are engaged; we own the sound of the violin; and we own our location; yet we are not focally aware of ourselves owning any of these components. But we *can* become focally aware of ourselves in relation to all of them if experience shifts from non-reflective to self-reflective. For instance, an ache in the periphery of the sensation component of experience might become focal as it increases in intensity. Our focus during the non-reflective experience is on the violin sound in the room (i.e. the environmental component). When the ache in our foot (let's say) becomes focal, experience immediately shifts to:

Cognition:	my foot hurts
Affect:	slight irritation
Behavior:	inclining head toward foot
Sensation:	pain in foot
Environ:	foot in room
"I":	ownership

In this self-reflective experience, the sensation component becomes the self-indicating component. It is that component that draws us to ourselves in relation to components of experience. Without a self-indicating component, we would not be aware of ourselves in relation to components of consciousness. A pain in our foot would not be experienced as a pain in our foot.

We might very well, though, be aware of the pain in our foot without being clearly aware of the pain or the foot being *ours*. This type of experience would look like this:

Cognition:	foot hurts
Affect:	slight irritation
Behavior:	inclining head toward foot
Sensation:	pain in foot
Environ:	foot in room
"I":	ownership

In this experience, we recognize that there is a sensation that one might call pain and that the pain is in a foot, but we wouldn't be clearly aware that the foot and the pain are ours. It would be as if we were referring to our own foot and pain from a third person point of view. These types of experiences characterize forms of dissociative experiences and experiences of brain damaged people. In this instance, the sensation component is either not a self-indicating component of consciousness, though it is owned [by us] (if the ownership can be focalized), or it is a self-indicating component that is deficient in strength. For instance, if someone were to ask us if our foot hurts, we would be able to affirm that it does even though we wouldn't feel the pain clearly, intimately and inextricably attached to us. We might display behavior that doesn't seem to match what we are saying but it would match the way we are saying it. We might appear somewhat dazed and confused.

If experience shifts from non-reflective to self-reflective with a (strong) self-indicating component, then the ownership which existed in peripheral consciousness shifts to focal consciousness and becomes cognitivized, while also remaining in peripheral consciousness, and we are clearly and intimately aware of the pain as ours. The cognitive component of consciousness would consist of the self-indicating component, which is the sensation of pain in foot (i.e. "hurt foot") and a cognitivized "I" (i.e. "my"). We would simultaneously own this component of consciousness. The ownership is the "I", which is never removed from peripheral consciousness, but split into itself as peripheral ownership and as cognitivized "I". So when we are self-reflective, we also own the self-reflection. Or, to put it another way, the cognitive component consists of a cognitivized "I" and a self-indicating component, and that whole cognitive component is owned. A self-reflective experience minus a cognitivized "I" would be similar to the dissociative experience above. That is, without the cognitivized "I", the self-indicating component, though focal, possesses little strength. We can connect it to ourselves, but not very clearly or intimately. We are to some degree dissociated from it. When the self-indicating component possesses a much greater strength than the cognitivized "I", then we are either hallucinating or engaged in a similar experience whereby the self-indicating component seems to take on environmental status.

For instance, a man who hears voices that aren't actually in the environment is engaged in an experience that would look like this:

	Real Self	False Self
Cognition:	["stay away from me"]	"stay away from her"
Affect:	[defensiveness]	ambivalence
Behavior:	[speaking forcefully]	unusual stare
Sensation:	[her]	voice of person
Environ:	[her in room]	voice of person in room
"I":	ownership	

In this experience, the real self consists of what the person would think, feel, do, and sense in that environment if he (let's say) were not hallucinating. The real self experience is simple, strong and right, but because of a history of rejection and distortion of the real self, the person hallucinating will protect the real self from more rejection and distortion with a false self. The cognition "get away from me" is the self-indicating component, but the "me" aspect of it (i.e. the cognitivized "I") is virtually gone. Instead of telling his mother (let's say) to stay away from him (because she is attacking the validity of his real self), he objectifies his own thought within the hallucination. He detaches or dissociates himself from his own thought and substitutes "her" for "me", which serves virtually to remove the cognitivized "I" from experience, leaving him with an over-powerful self-indicating component. The thought becomes 'real', out there, in the environment. The hallucination, in effect, protects his real self from annihilation by over-strengthening the self-indicating component (the thought itself) while virtually eliminating the cognitivized "I".

- **Stern's Emergent and Core Selves: The Emergent Self**

Daniel Stern's notions of emergent and core selves, which he has developed in relation to both the psychoanalytic and the developmental psychology traditions, comes close to the experientialist theory's notion of self. It clarifies and rectifies some of the nebulousness and errors, respectively, of the stages of development as propounded by ego psychology, and it better accommodates the holistic and analytic nature of experientialist theory.

Stern argues that infants experience the world in a much more definite manner than is described in ego psychology's autistic phase of development (0 to 2 months). Studies show that infants seek sensory stimulation and one of their most important stimuli is the human face. Infants have distinct biases or preferences in regard to sensations, and these preferences show all the signs of being innate. Also, infants appear to have a central tendency to form and test hypotheses about what is occurring in the world (Bruner, 1977). They seem constantly to be "evaluating," in the sense of asking, is this different from or the same as that? Stern concludes that infants will use this central tendency to rapidly categorize the social world into conforming and contrasting patterns, events, sets, and experiences. In addition to this, Stern argues that affective and cognitive processes cannot be readily separated. In simple learning tasks, activation builds up and falls off, indicating that cognitive learning is affect-laden. Similarly, in an intense affective moment, perception and cognition go on (Stern, 1985).

Stern sees the development of a self occurring in process from day one of the infant's life. He argues that an infant "can experience the process of emerging organization as well as the result," and that it is this experience of emerging organization that he calls the emergent sense of self (Stern, 1985). Stern is emphatic in asserting that infants do not experience non-organization (as is claimed in the autistic phase of development in ego psychology). Rather, infants experience things in the world with exquisite clarity and vividness, and that the lack of relatedness between these experiences is not noticed. As these diverse experiences become somehow yoked or associated with each other, the infant experiences the emergence of organization. The sense of an emergent self concerns the process and product of forming organization. Stern believes that infants can not only organize their environments, but, importantly, they can experience the organization of these experiences. It is out of the *experience* of organizing sense experiences that an emerging self occurs. Stern concludes that "the sense of an emergent self thus includes two components, the products of forming relations between isolated experiences and the process" (Stern, 1985).

If we were to convert Stern's notion of an emergent self, up to this point, into the experientialist theory, we would hold that the sensory experiences had by the infant are, by definition, multi-componential structures in addition to being comparatively discrete or separate. That is, an infant, like an adult, will not only sense aspects of its environment and be selective about those aspects, but it will also cognize, feel, and behave within an environment. According to Stern, infants show a seemingly innate ability to perceive amodally, i.e. to take information received in one sensory modality and translate it into another sensory modality. For example, an infant will respond in similar ways to light intensity and sound intensity. It is as if the infant is hard-wired to respond in a similar manner to intensity, whether that intensity is visual, auditory, tactile, etc. In addition to this capacity, according to Stern and developmental research, infants show signs of being innately able to cross sensory modalities and integrate information from several modalities at the same time. For example, an infant will cognize congruity between a voice and lips moving. Studies show that when the two are not in sync, the infant will show behavioral signs of preferring to look at the integrated voice-lips vs. the unintegrated voice-lips. Stern argues that at a preverbal level of consciousness, the experience of finding a cross-modal match (especially the first time) would feel like a correspondence or imbuing of present experience with something prior or familiar, a form of déjà vu event. Here, Stern is positing an affective component in relation to a sensory and cognitive component. That is, matching sensory modalities is a cognitive function, and this cognitive function (cognition) is connected to an affective component (form of déjà vu). If we simply add the behavioral component (comportment) of the infant's looking behavior and the behavioral component (physiology) of the infant's heart rate or other bodily activity in relation to the environmental stimuli, then we will have the consciousness structure of experience. If we add to this an emerging sense of self, we will have an experiential structure.

A question arises at this point: Can an infant have a discreet sensory experience without cognitive, affective, behavioral and environmental components attached to it? Can an infant sense something without feeling it in some way, acting in relation to it in some way, and physiologically responding to it in some way? Though Stern does not say this, his analysis of developmental studies is couched in multi-componential language. He seems to be operating within the traditional scientific linear model of theorizing by concentrating on sensation of the environment first, then moving to cognition, affect and behavior, but the language of his analyses borders on holistic and experiential theorizing. He links sensation with affect, while implying a type of cognitive function, as noted above; he links proprioception (i.e. feeling of one's own bodily existence and motions) with visual sensation by demonstrating how infants can "know" specific configurations of other people's faces by moving its face in a similar manner, and he, through Heinz Werner (1948) links sensation with affect in the phenomenon of "physiognomic" perception, or associating visual images (e.g. squiggles, smooth lines turning down, and jagged lines) with various feelings (e.g. happy, sad and angry). Such language seems to push the scientific linear model to its edge where it borders on transformation. The experientialist theory pushes the language over the edge into a holistic understanding of the self and reality.

Another important idea of Stern's is his notion of "vitality affects." Vitality affects are more globalized feelings that go beyond sensory-laden ideas such as intensity level, motion, number, and rhythm and yet are not as discreet as the categorical affects of anger, sadness, happiness, etc. These are feelings like "surging," "fading away," "fleeting," "explosive," "crescendo," "decrescendo," "bursting," "drawn out," etc. These vitality affects are experienced not only by the infant but also by the adult, and they can be communicated between infant and adult and felt between person and object. For instance, these affects can be communicated by how a mother picks up a baby, felt in how the mother folds the diapers, felt and communicated by how mother grooms her hair or the baby's hair, reaches for a bottle, unbuttons her blouse, etc.

These more subtle forms of feelings correspond nicely with the peripheral (and sometimes focal) aspects of experiential structures and play a vital role in the maintenance of SSR structures and a self-deceptive role in complex structures. For instance, a mother who picks up her baby roughly while believing that she is behaving in a gentle, loving manner, would be communicating the roughness to the child while contradicting that roughness by smiling (falsely). The infant, if we are to agree with Stern, can experience the contradiction between the roughness and the smiling and might have difficulty integrating these two inconsistent modalities. In this example then, a mother is communicating a complex structure within which she is participating to the infant, and the infant might either disregard the inconsistency (as it does in the voice-lips studies) or somehow accommodate the inconsistency. This problem is compounded once the child gains more knowledge of smiling faces being consistent with certain types of touch. The rough touch does not match the smiling face and the child's experience is conflicted. If the self is emerging throughout these interactive processes, then the emerging self is being affected, influenced or in some sense determined by the consistent (authentic) or inconsistent (inauthentic) behavior of the parent. This notion is consistent with the experiential notion of SSR structures (authenticity) being either confirmed by others (mutual consistency), disconfirmed by others (conflicting SSR structures), or distorted by others (rejecting the rightness of one's structure). When mother smiles while handling her infant roughly, her experience could be analyzed in this fashion:

Cognition:	[I'm frustrated with you]	I'm bad for feeling frustrated	I'm acting lovingly
Affect:	[frustration]	self-rejection	false affection
Behavior:	[rough handling]	look down	false smile
Sensation:	[baby]	baby	baby
Environ:	[room]	room	room
"I":	[ownership]		

The baby is able to experience the surging and explosive quality of the mother's handling without necessarily understanding it as evidence of anger (vitality affect) while virtually simultaneously experiencing the drawn out pacifying smile on the mother's face. Being confronted with these inconsistent experiences, the infant might well have difficulty integrating them.

One way Stern characterizes vitality affects as different from categorical affects is by locating them within motivational states, appetites, and tensions. They are connected to the vital processes of the organism, e.g. breathing, hunger, elimination, falling asleep and waking up, feeling the coming and going of emotions and thoughts, etc. Again, the language links experiential components where breathing is categorized as a form of physiological behavior or body movement (sometimes comportment when done purposefully), hunger a sensation, elimination a combination of behavior and environment, falling asleep and waking up as forms of comportment closely associated with physiological movement, feeling the coming of emotions and thoughts as subtle types of affect, etc. Vital feelings are the feelings associated with all of these vital processes. They can serve to fill the affective component of a given experiential structure.

In the last example, the vital affect can either precede a categorical affect or it can underlie the affect. So for Stern, vital affects and categorical affects are two types of affect that can co-occur. One reason Stern distinguishes these two types of affect is because, he argues, vitality affects cannot be accounted for simply by the notion of levels of activation. That is, the organism's sensory apparatus (organs plus nervous system) can be activated causing activation contours, but such activation is not the same thing as 'feelings'. The 'feelings' associated with these activation contours are not the same thing as the activation contours themselves. So a person can experience a rush of thoughts and 'feel' that rush as well as 'think' the thoughts. Experientially, this distinction makes perfect sense if we are distinguishing between cognition (thoughts) and affect (surging, bursting, etc.), but to distinguish them from other affects is more questionable unless we are using vital affects to conflict with categorical affects (as in the above example) or unless we include the vital affects as peripheral components in relation to the categorical affects. For instance, we could feel happy focally and a surging or bursting vital affect peripherally within the same experience.

For Stern the self is somehow generated within the process of organizing experience in relation to its environment, especially an environment containing human beings. Studies show that infants tend to scan the edges or boundaries of the objects in their environment, but with human beings, they will look within the boundaries of the person's head, at facial features. The social or interpersonal connection to the formation of the self occurs in the first few months of human life.

Stern argues that "there is no reason to give any one domain of experience primacy and make it the point of departure to approach the infant's organization of experience. Several approaches can be described, all of them valid, all of them necessary, and all of them equally "primary." Included in these experiential approaches are: 1 the infant's action: "self generated actions and sensations are primary experiences," 2) pleasure and unpleasure (hedonic tone), ala Freud, 3) discrete categories of affect, 4) infant states of consciousness, e.g. drowsiness, alert activity, fuzz-cry, sleep, etc., and 5) perceptions and cognition (the route of most experimentalists) (Stern, 1985).

Experientially, the infant's actions and sensations fall under the components of behavior and sensation respectively; pleasure and unpleasure fall under the component of affect, perceptions and cognitions fall under sensations and environment (perception of external things, including one's own body) and cognition. States of consciousness are understood as descriptions of types of experiential structures rather than primary experiences. Sleep can be eliminated from 'primary experience' because it is not actually experienced; its existence is inferred from evidence in conscious states. Drowsiness and other conscious states are actually experiential structures whose contents include drowsiness features.

Aside from the problem with consciousness and an implied rather than explicit connection with a physical environment (indicators of the scientific linear mind-set), Stern's conception of the infant's experience and that of an emerging self are very close to a holistic experientialist conception of reality. What remains for our discussion is Stern's sense of a core self.

- **Stern's Emergent and Core Selves: The Core Self**

As an infant grows and interaction with its environment increases, a core self is formed. A core self includes: 1) self-agency or authorship of one's own actions, 2) self-coherence or having a sense of being a non-fragmented, physical whole with boundaries and a locus of integrated action, 3) self-affectivity or experiencing patterned inner qualities of feeling that belong with other experiences of self, and 4) self-history or having the sense of enduring, of a continuity with one's own past. The primacy of interpersonal experience is evident within the first two months of the infant's life, and primarily out of this interpersonal experience comes a sense of a core self and core others. This process, according to Stern, does not happen over two years, ending with an individuation stage of development, as argued in ego psychology, but rather within two to seven months after birth. The infant does not have to go through a symbiotic stage, then hatching, practicing, and rapprochement stages purported by ego psychologists to reach a sense of a core self; the core self is forming within two to seven months from birth and, as explained already, is emerging earlier on than that.

For Stern "a sense of core self results from the integration of these four basic self-experiences into a social subjective perspective." The sense of a core self is thus an experiential sense of events" (Stern, 1985). For example, when an infant closes its eyes, the world gets dark. At first, an infant might not be aware of itself closing its eyes; it just closes its eyes. But it is aware of the sensation of closing its eyes, or of the burning sensation in its eyes that prompts it to close its eyes; it is aware of the relief (pleasure) of closing its eyes; it is also aware of the darkness that occurs when it closes its eyes; and it is already capable of crossing sensory modes (seeing, touching, etc.) And it is already interconnected in terms of sensation, cognition, affect, and behavior (at least in rudimentary terms). Out of this conglomeration of experiential interconnectivity comes a sense of a core self.

Specifically, according to Stern, agency can be broken down into three possible invariants of experience: 1) the sense of volition that precedes a motor act, 2) the proprioceptive feedback that does or does not occur during the act, and 3) the predictability of the consequences that follow the act. Stern believes that the invariant of volition is the most fundamental invariant of the core self experience. It is some 'mental registration' (usually outside of awareness) of an 'action plan', e.g. suck, gaze, etc. The physical action follows from the mental action plan. Stern argues that acts that occur above the level of reflexes are not simply performed by chance or accident; rather, they are preceded by some sort of action plan or mental representation, no matter how fleeting that plan might be.

For example, if a subject is asked to sign his name on a paper and then on a blackboard, the signatures will appear very similar though it can be shown that different groups of muscles are used to complete each act. This points to the idea that there exists some sort of mental 'action plan' that is executed by different parts of the body to produce similar results. This notion of action plans is similar to Piaget's and Beck's notion of cognitive schemas, and it falls neatly within the scientific linear conception of reality.

Experientially, cognitions do not precede action; rather, they co-occur with action (behavior). The 'action plan', if within experience, registers either in focal or peripheral cognition. If focal, the infant (or adult) is clearly aware of it, and the strength of the structure is relatively strong. If peripheral, the infant's awareness of it is less clear, and the strength of the structure is relatively weak. If it occurs outside of experience within which the infant participates, then its existence is inconsequential in relation to the infant. It is equivalent to non-existent. It may very well be consequential in relation to those who are interacting with the infant, those conceiving of the notion of 'action plans' in relation to infant (and adult) behavior, but if such 'action plans' occur outside of infant awareness, then their existence cannot be connected to a developing core self because there is nothing being experientially processed by the infant. Processes are occurring in the infant from another person's perspective (e.g. researcher's), but to claim that the infant's developing core self depends upon processes of which the infant is completely unaware, without owning that claim, is to create a meta-experiential construct, or to distort reality. In order for Stern's notion of 'action plan' to carry experiential weight, it must either be experienced in some way (focally or peripherally) by the infant or believed in by the infant through trusting another person. And, of course, since this trust cannot be the product of theoretical exchange, it seems that it needs to be the result of basic interaction between infant and adult. So the notion of 'action plan' might contribute directly to the behavior of the researcher, but to the infant it means only what is being communicated through the experiential structures within which the researcher is participating.

Experientially, Stern's notion of 'action plan' is similar to Beck's notion of 'cognitive schema', and the same analysis can be applied to each. An 'action plan' is a cognition, and cognitions occur in conjunction with behaviors, not in a prerequisite or semi-causative role. An analysis of it would look like this:

Cognition: suck thumb (pre-linguistic)
Affect: anticipated pleasure
Behavior: body preparing to move
Sensation: body, environ
Environ: room
("I"):   ownership
      SSR

which changes to:
Cognition: moving thumb to mouth (pre-linguistic)
Affect: confidence
Behavior: moving thumb toward mouth
Sensation: body, environment
Environ: room
("I")   ownership
      SSR

which ends in:
Cognition: sucking thumb (pre-linguistic)
Affect: pleasure
Behavior: sucking
Sensation: thumb, environment
Environ: room

("I"):   ownership
          SSR

This analysis argues that there is no 'action plan' that precedes the action but rather that several relatively discreet experiences occur in relation to each other. The 'action plan' notion is actually a cognitive component of the initial experience. It is accompanied by the behavior of the body's preparation to move. In other words, there already exists an action or a behavior prior to the behavior of moving the thumb toward the mouth; it is the body preparing itself to alter its current movements. As the thumb moves toward the mouth, a new cognition occurs: moving thumb toward mouth (pre-linguistic). Here the infant cognizes its own body motion. It is confident in relation to this motion. If the thumb should miss the mouth and therefore conflict with the anticipated pleasure felt in the initial experience, then slight irritation might occur and slightly diminished confidence, along with a continuation or persistence of motion toward the mouth (until the skill is learned into habit).

The initial experiential structure is strong enough to prompt the next structure, and there are no conflicting experiential structures vying for expression, e.g. the infant is not attending to a pain in its foot, which might bypass thumb sucking and move directly into crying. The prompting of movement of the thumb toward the mouth is already happening in the prior experience where the body is preparing to move. Whether the movement of the thumb toward the mouth occurs or not is not a function of volition (will); rather, it is a function of experience. If the experience is strong enough and there are no significantly strong conflicting experiential structures (and these seem to be reciprocal notions, i.e. strength to alter flow of current experience depends upon strength of conflicting experiences), then the act will occur.

Viewed in this way, volition is not a mental phenomenon that somehow converts mentality into physical movement; rather, it is either a meta-experiential construct or a short-cut way of referring to an experiential process. If the former, it will be rejected by experientialism; if the latter, it will be accepted as an effective heuristic concept.

Stern's second invariant property of proprioceptive feedback converts nicely into contents of peripheral experience and focal experience when a skill is first being learned. The infant will initiate movement of its thumb toward its mouth and be peripherally aware of the accuracy of its movement through proprioceptive feedback. Experientially, proprioceptive feedback consists of a set of experiences in relation to the task at hand. Initial learning might entail confidence-persistence-irritation experiences until the skill becomes automatic; then confidence will prevail and become peripheral.

Stern's third invariant is consequence of action. This also converts nicely into experiential structures. It refers to the experiences that follow a given act. For instance, if the movement of the thumb to the mouth is successful and is followed by various sense-pleasure experiences, then the infant can begin to recognize the efficacy of moving its body. The pleasure reinforces its efforts and helps create a sense of a core self.

In converting Stern's notion of agency into experiential theory, an initial thumb sucking experiential structure might look like this:

Cognition: this is agitating (pre-linguistic)
Affect: agitation
Behavior: body moving in agitated fashion
Sensation: body (hunger possibly), environ
Environ: room
("I"):   ownership
      SSR
which changes to:
Cognition: suck thumb (pre-linguistic)
Affect: urge
Behavior: body preparing to move
Sensation: body, environ
Environ: room
("I"):   ownership
      SSR
which changes to:
Cognition: moving thumb to mouth (pre-linguistic)
Affect: confidence
Behavior: moving thumb toward mouth
Sensation: body, environment
Environ: room
("I")   ownership

SSR
which ends in:

Cognition:	sucking thumb (pre-linguistic)
Affect:	pleasure
Behavior:	sucking
Sensation:	thumb, environment
Environ:	room
("I"):	ownership

    SSR

If we posit that the initial urge for an infant to suck its thumb is innate, possibly generalized from the innate sucking of the nipple, and is prompted by some form of bodily agitation or discomfort (e.g. hunger, etc.), then we can locate agency within the cognitive component of experience rather than the mind. Agency becomes a property of experience and splitting experience into cognition (mind) and behavior (body) is either unnecessary or misleading.

The signature example above can be explained without resorting to a mind before body (linear) explanation. For instance, each experiential set accounting for each type of signature (i.e. desk vs. board) consists of its own set of components. They might look like this:

Cognition:	sign name on desk	: sign name on board
Affect:	confidence	: confidence
Behavior:	body preparing to sign	: body preparing to sign
Sensation:	pen, desk	: chalk, board
Environ:	room	: room
("I"):	ownership	: ownership

    SSR   SSR

Cognition:	signing name on desk	: signing name on board
Affect:	confidence	: confidence
Behavior:	body signing	: body signing
Sensation:	pen, desk	: chalk, board
Environ:	room	: room
("I"):	ownership	: ownership

    SSR   SSR

Cognition:	completed signature	: completed signature
Affect:	confidence	: confidence
Behavior:	looking at signature	: looking at signature

Sensation:	pen, desk	: chalk, board
Environ:	room	: room
("I"):	ownership	: ownership
SSR		SSR

If we can assume that the desk signature preceded the board signature and that the person already knows how the signature looks and feels during and after he signs it, then we can hypothesize that his proprioceptive feedback can sufficiently inform him that his board signature is 'right' (close in appearance to his desk signature). The muscles used are not different enough to produce dissimilar signatures. But all he might have to do is sign his name with his other hand to show that any 'action plan' or 'cognitive schema', if present, is either very faulty in its conversion to action or that it will take time and practice to get one signature to look like the other. If the former is the case, then an 'action plan' seems to be a relatively impotent notion, and if the latter is the case, then 'action plan' can be replaced altogether by a learning explanation, i.e. recognizing how one's signature looks and feels and making sure a new signature looks and feels similarly.

So rather than locate volition (agency) within an 'action plan', which is located within the mind, and which precedes an action, experientialism locates it within the cognitive component of experience, which is inextricably connected to the other components, and which co-occurs with behavior and evolves into other experiential structures, also, possibly, containing agency.

Stern argues that self-coherence helps develop a core self in an infant. Self-coherence is established by determining a unity of locus, coherence of motion, coherence of temporal structure, coherence of intensity structure and coherence of form. Briefly, the unity of locus refers to the idea that "a coherent entity ought to be in one place at one time, and its various actions should emanate from one locus" (Stern, 1985). Coherence of motion refers to the idea that things that move coherently in time belong together. Coherence of temporal structure refers to the idea that many behaviors that are performed simultaneously by one person share a common temporal structure. Coherence of intensity structure refers to the idea that behavioral intensities of one person generally match the intensities of another.

Coherence of form refers to the idea that one's form or configuration "belongs" to oneself or another.

So the notion of coherence applies to both the infant and to other persons (or entities). An infant can recognize coherent patterns of behavior, affect, and sensations within itself and in relation to others and is able to differentiate these patterns as discrete. The self-other differentiation occurs early in life as these patterns are recognized and matched between the infant and others. For instance, infants are able "to conserve the identity of a particular face across the various transformations of that face in different facial expressions" (Stern, 1985). They are able to keep track of the identity of an object in spite of changes in size or distance, its orientation or position of presentation, its degree of shading, etc.

In addition to self-coherence, Stern argues that self-affectivity is critical in helping form the core self. Self-affectivity refers to the emotions felt by the infant and how these emotions are separated into discrete categories. Stern argues that each emotion consists of three invariants: 1) proprioceptive feedback from face, respiration, vocal aspects, etc., 2) arousal or activation, and 3) emotion-specific qualities of feeling. For instance, parents and others can communicate joy to an infant by making faces, tossing it up in the air and catching it, playing with it, smiling, laughing, etc. The infant will respond in kind.

Eckman's (1971) studies of adult human beings indicate that emotional expressions seem to be universal, i.e. that all humans know how to feel discrete emotions and recognize them in others. Apply the same notion to infants and we have an affective and innate form of core self development. Infants can recognize their own emotions and others' emotions through expressions of those emotions by others and proprioceptive feedback within themselves.

Finally, self-history refers to the ability of infants (and adults) to remember the other core self invariants: agency, coherence and affect. They are able to connect things they've done in the past (agency), with discrete and understandable sets of experience (coherence), and with their feelings connected to themselves and others. Memory gives continuity to other core self invariants. It locates infants (and adults) in time and space over time.

All of these core self invariants discussed by Stern, for the exception of those aspects of agency already discussed, fit well into the experiential analysis of reality.

The relationship between the caregiver(s) and the infant is crucial in the development of the core self and the core other. The infant's attention, curiosity and cognitive engagement with the world are regulated by both the infant and the caregiver. Both respond to each other; the relationship is reciprocal but not symmetrical, i.e. the caregiver can stimulate the interest of the infant, and the infant's interest can stimulate the interest of the caregiver, but the caregiver brings much more experience to the interaction than does the infant. The same applies to the satiation of interest and involvement.

Again, these interactions, according to Stern, are relatively discrete. The core self of the infant forms in relation to a process composed of relatively discrete experiences and not through alternating fusion and separation states in relation to the caregiver as posited by ego psychology.

Developmental psychology's integration with psychoanalytic and attachment theory seem to have produced a theory of self that aligns quite well with the ideas constituting the notion of self in experientialist theory. In experientialist theory the notion of "I" as ownership refers to the cognitive linkage between one's thoughts, feelings, behaviors, sensations and one's own body as the object of sensations as one's own, i.e. "mine". Though neither experientialist nor Stern's developmental/psychoanalytic theory addresses exactly how the "mine" cognition occurs in infancy, Stern's theory of emergent self comes close. As interactions with one's environment, especially the caregivers in one's environment, occur, the infant is able to process these interactions and develop a distinct core self and a distinct core other. Symbiotic and separation stages are replaced or analyzed into relatively discrete experiences involving at first sensual representations, intensities, rhythms, physiognomic perceptions and vitality affects (emerging self) that eventually help form a variety of self-invariants which integrate to form a core self.

Viewed through an experientialist lens, the infant engages in numerous SSR experiences very early in life. Though it is unclear as to how exactly the infant comes to own self-indicating components of consciousness (e.g. my 'thumb', my 'hunger', my 'pain', etc.), it seems that it does so at a very early age and primarily in conjunction with a caregiver. Those experiences that Stern refers to as self-regulated by the infant (interest moving to satiation moving to irritation, etc.) are representative of SSR experiences and are, experientially, when integrated, the core self.

For example, when an infant is interested in a caregiver's face, its attention is on that face. When the caregiver responds in kind to the infant, then the infant's interest experience is confirmed by the caregiver. In effect, the caregiver is approving the rightness of the infant's experience. The infant's core self, realized in the SSR structure of its interest experience, is strengthened and affirmed by the SSR structure of the caregiver's interest experience. But when the infant's interest experience is not responded to in kind, then the infant's core self is not confirmed, though it might not be rejected. The caregiver might not be in the mood to confirm the interest experience of the infant. Hence, the experience plays itself out and the infant's attention shifts. But if the caregiver rejects the interest experience of the infant and communicates something like, "Oh, don't look at me, you terrible baby," then the rightness of the experiential structure is rejected, and the infant's core self is subject to alteration. As far as the infant is concerned (we'll hypothesize), it's interest in the caregiver is a sincere expression of *who the infant is* at this time; as such, it is SSR, real, and good. But when the caregiver rejects the legitimacy of the experiential structure within which the infant participates, then the immediate response would be something like:

Cognition:	this behavior, feeling, etc. is wrong? (pre-linguistic)
Affect:	confusion
Behavior:	slightly puzzled look
Sensation:	caregiver
Environ:	room
"I":	ownership

which eventually shifts to (after repeated like experiences):

Cognition:	this behavior, feeling, etc. is wrong (pre-linguistic)
Affect:	self-rejection
Behavior:	vacant stare
Sensation:	caregiver
Environ:	room
"I":	ownership

The rightness of the infant's experience is rejected by the caregiver and the infant is made to respond as if its natural (sincere) self-expression is wrong. Since it experiences its experience as perfectly right, the infant is initially confused in relation to the caregiver's response. Because of the disparity in power between the caregiver and the infant, the infant can do little more than adjust to the caregiver's rejection of the rightness of its experiential structure (it's self), accepting the caregiver's rejection and denying its own self-acceptance. Its experiential structure becomes complex and its identity is distorted.

If Stern is correct about the early development of a self in infancy, and experiential theory is correct about the formation of complex structures, then false self structures can form very early in life, thus creating emotional dependencies upon caregivers in the form of identity alterations due to, in this case, emotional or psychological abuse. Add to this physical and sexual abuse and we have the rudiments for the development of a variety of psychological disorders and identity distortions that might not yet be accounted for in psychiatric nosology.

- **Experiential Consistency and the Self**

In experientialist terms, emotional consistency means the ability for mother (or various other nurturing people) to confirm the rightness of the experiences within which the child participates. She must be able to confirm the rightness of her own experience while confirming the rightness of the child's experience, and for mothers who, themselves, have difficulty confirming the rightness of their own experience or who tend to misjudge the rightness of the experiential structures within which they participate while promoting the continuation of mixed or complex experiential structures, the task of confirming the rightness of the child's experiences becomes very difficult, resulting in increased inconsistency within the self of the mother, the self of the child, and the relationship between the mother and child.

At this stage of development, the identity of the child is maintained not only through the consistent confirming responses of the mother and other caregivers but also through the consistent confirmations of the child itself. Again, this consistency can be established via interactions with other caregivers or through the individual confirmations by the child itself. A child may be able to withstand, ward off, or absorb some instances of mother-rejection as long as it has some integrity of self established on its own terms or in relation to others.

- ### *An Experiential Being*

An experiential being is someone who works out of SSR structures, an authentic person, divested of any complexity. As a child is forming its core self, it tends to express itself as an experiential being. It acts in accordance with its own determinations; the experiential structure within which it operates is simple, strong and right; the morality or rightness of its actions is not questioned or doubted; the actions are natural to the child. The componential structure of the experiences within which the child participates is consistent. He or she *is who he or she is in that situation.*

When a person acts as an experiential being and the person's self is confirmed by someone else, e.g. adult caregiver, then the SSR structure is confirmed and the person's identity is strengthened. The simplicity of the structure remains intact, the strongness is strengthened, and the rightness is confirmed.

The person's SSR structure can be disconfirmed when the other person (often the adult care-giver) rejects the rightness of the person's structure.

A rejection of a person's structure differs from a disagreement with the cognitive content of that structure, or a discordant feeling in relation to that structure, or the disapproval of the behavior of that structure, or a lack of appreciation of the sensations of that structure, or a lack of congruency in relation to the environment of that structure. One person, for instance, can disagree with the belief (cognitive content) of another and yet accept that person as a person and respect their belief even when it differs from one's own. One person might not be able to understand the emotional expression of another given a certain situation without characterizing the other as inferior, abnormal, or sub-human. A mother might reject the behavior of her child without rejecting the child himself. One person might be unable to understand the sensual experiences of another without determining that the other is abnormal, defective, or sub-human. And one person might not understand why another person accepts or fits into an environment that the person finds ill-suited to him without characterizing that person as bad, evil or wrong.

But when rejection entails the rejection of another person as a person, or the objectification of that person, or the demonization of that person, or the sub-human characterization of that person, then rejection can prompt the formation of complex structures.

As explained in Section 2 (Compound and Complex Structures), complex structures tend to be formed when people in positions of power over others are able to impose their wills, wishes, and values upon others by altering their identity structure. The imposition of a value and the inculcation of that value within the other person through repeated acts of imposition or sometimes single acts of trauma prompt the formation of complex structures consisting of a false self that covers or is superimposed upon a real self.

The distinction between non-rejecting, non-confirming responses and rejecting, disconfirming responses might be difficult to discern. The passive father might have trouble dealing with a naturally active or aggressive daughter. His frustrations might lead him to think that something is wrong with or abnormal about his daughter. But if the daughter is working out of, or participating in, SSR structures, then there is nothing wrong with or abnormal about her. That is who she is, and who she is needs to be accepted by the father. His efforts to 'make her normal' can prompt the development of a complex structure in the experiential (and identity) structure of the daughter if she denies the rightness of her own structure and accepts the characterization of her by the father. She will come to view herself as abnormal. If she is capable of accepting the legitimacy of her own response to her father's attempts to characterize her as abnormal and to assertively confront her father by letting him know that she is unwilling to accept his characterization or judgment of her as abnormal, then the father is in position to grapple with her assertive confrontation. This grappling process is often times painful and people attempt to avoid going through it. It often means that the characterizations or judgments made by people, judgments that seem quite accurate to them, must be rejected. This often entails an admission of being wrong, narrow-minded, small-hearted, or incompetent, an admission difficult for most if not all people to make.

This process of accepting the legitimacy of one's own experiential structure (or, in this case, feelings of hurt, irritation, confusion, resentment, anger, etc. over being characterized as abnormal), followed by one's assertive confrontation in relation to another's trying to impose his determinations (will, values, etc.) upon oneself, which, optimally, will lead to the grappling process within the experiential structure of the person attempting the imposition, is referred to as the *process of moralitization*, or making moral.

In our example, the father tries to impose his value upon his daughter because he has difficulty dealing with his daughter's behavior. He has difficulty accepting his daughter as she is. Therefore, he tries to impose his values upon her by characterizing her as abnormal and acting upon that characterization, thus communicating to her that she is abnormal. Her experience of her experience is not consistent with that of her father. Therefore, she will tend to respond initially to her father's characterization (rejection) of her with confusion or disorientation. As far as she is concerned, she is acting in a wholly normal and natural manner. And if the experiential structure is simple, strong and right, she *is* acting in a normal, natural manner.

If this confusion or disorientation prompts hurt, irritation, resentment, and/or anger experiences, then she is in position to assertively confront her father. If she is capable of doing so, she will let her father know that his characterization of her is hurtful and wrong, that this is who she is, and her father will be left to grapple with the assertive confrontation.

But more often than not, in situations where there is a natural power differential (e.g. parent-child situations), the child is incapable of or unable to make such assertive confrontations. The child is in a dependent relationship with the parent in many ways: emotionally, psychologically, physically, economically, etc. Therefore, the child is ill-equipped to assertively confront the parent in an effective manner. So the child well tend toward denying the legitimacy of its own structure and creating a false self to cover up its real self in order to continue living and surviving in the current situation. When the false self is congruent with the values of the imposing care-giver, then the child has successfully adapted to values of another and life will be more tolerable for it, though complex. The child's experiential status at this point will change from SSR (experiential being) to complex (distorted reality, not an experiential being) at least in regard to the issue at hand.

The imposition of one person's values, will, wishes, etc. upon another is, in this work, considered to be a form of abuse. It can be emotional (or psychological), physical, or sexual in nature. It is to be distinguished from learning. Accepting the values of another through learning is fundamentally different from accepting the values of another through imposition or force. Learning entails a trust in the caring of another for one's own well-being. The learner trusts the teacher in regard to what he or she is learning because she realizes that what she is learning is for her own good. Accepting the values of another when that value is imposed upon oneself entails the rejection of one's own experiential structure in favor of that of the other. It entails the rejection of oneself and the accommodation of oneself to another, and this entails a mistrust of the intentions of the supposed teacher. The teacher becomes boss or master, and the student becomes employee or slave. A false self is adopted in order to deal with one's own self-rejection and one's interpersonal situation. A dominant:submissive relationship is formed (at least in the given area of concern) and a fundamental unit of a meta-experiential structure obtains.

Let's use an example to elaborate upon the above contentions. Junior, a two-year old toddler, is curious about a light socket on the wall. His experiential structure could be represented thus:

Cognition: What's that?
Affect: curiosity
Behavior: moving to put finger into light socket
Sensation: light socket
Environ: room
                SSR

At this point Junior's experience is perfectly normal, right, and good, i.e. simple, strong, and right. He is naturally curious. He doesn't question whether or not his behavior is right or wrong; he assumes that it is right; he is simply acting in accord with his curiosity. He is totally unaware of the possible consequences to him of his action.

Mother sees Junior and is instantly fearful. She rushes to him and pulls him away from the light socket. Mother doesn't question whether or not her feelings of fear or her behavior of pulling Junior away from the light socket is right or wrong; she assumes that it's right. She accepts the legitimacy of both her fear experience and her pulling-him-away-from-the-light-socket experience. Her pulling him away is an assertive confrontation.

Junior flails a bit, not wanted to have his behavior stopped and the satisfaction of his curiosity impeded or prevented. Mother might at this point question her behavior, e.g. Am I too rough? Am I hurting him? But let's say that she grapples with her own assertive confrontation in the wake of Junior's flailing response and affirms its legitimacy.

Now Junior is in position to grapple with mother's assertive confrontation (pulling him away from light socket). In the grappling process, which might take several assertive confrontations on mother's part, Junior 're-organizes' or 're-creates' himself in relation to his environment. He realizes, based on his trust of mother, that his behavior might hurt him and that light sockets are not a proper object of his curiosity, or at least that his current methods of expressing that curiosity are not in his best interest and that mother is right. Mother has set limits on Junior's behavior, but she has not challenged or rejected Junior himself. She does not explicitly or implicitly convey to him that he is bad, wrong, evil, abnormal, or sub-human. She confronts his behavior and not who he is. She does not reject the rightness of the structure within which Junior participates.

In this interaction mother's experiential structures are SSR. She accepts the legitimacy of feeling fear in relation to Junior's behavior, she accepts the legitimacy of her method of assertive confrontation, and she allows Junior to grapple with her assertive confrontation.

Junior's experiential structures are SSR. He accepts the legitimacy of his curiosity experience, he accepts the legitimacy of his flailing experience, though his flailing experience conflicts with mother's pulling-him-away experience, and he ultimately accepts the legitimacy of his acceptance-of-limitations experience, i.e. his learning experience. Junior has learned not to do something in the world and his identity is intact. He remains an experiential being.

Father, on the other hand, operates differently from mother. Upon seeing Junior reach for the light socket, he immediately feels fear, but he doesn't accept the legitimacy of it; rather, he rejects its legitimacy because he has sustained a history of complexity. He has been *complexified* since youth, i.e. he has been told that boys are weak if they feel and show fear. He has in the past denied the rightness of his own fear experiences and replaced them with aggressive experiences, i.e. a false self. So instead of pulling Junior away from the light socket, father hits Junior and calls him an idiot for sticking his finger in the light socket. Like mother, father's action might have to be repeated before Junior responds the way he wants him to respond.

Junior's experiential structure in relation to father can be represented in this way:

Cognition:	[What's that?]	I'm bad?	I'm bad.	I'm acting good
Affect:	[curious]	confusion	self-rejection	false confidence
Behavior:	[finger in socket]	puzzled look	looking down	false compliance
Sensation:	[light socket]	father's hand, etc.	father, room	father, room
Environ:	[room]	room	room	room
	SSR – Real Self			**False Self**

In this experiential structure, Junior's curious experience represents his real self. He questions his experience and his identity when father hits him and calls him a name, indicating that he is in some way bad, wrong, stupid, etc. Junior's initial response to father's behavior is one of confusion or a type of disorientation. What he accepted unconditionally as right (i.e. his curiosity experience) is being rejected by a person who has considerable power over him. After repeated exposures to this physically and emotionally abusive behavior, and because Junior is dependent upon his father in many ways, Junior denies the validity of his own experiential structure, a structure that is SSR, and accepts the value imposed upon him by his father. He accepts that he is bad, wrong or stupid, and then he constructs a false self that will be acceptable to father. In this instance, we have him becoming docile and compliant with father's wishes. Later in life, possibly, father will no longer have to hit Junior to get him to do what he wants him to do; a simple name calling might do the trick, or even a simple threatening or pejorative look.

Junior has developed a complex structure in relation to father and his identity is distorted. His dependency upon father now extends from natural emotional, psychological and economic dependence to include a distorted form of dependence: they have developed a dominant:submissive relationship. Father dominates Junior because Junior has, in effect, lost or buried that aspect of himself that was real (his curiosity experience), and Junior becomes submissive to father. This is another example of the Rousseauean idea of masters and slaves, when force is turned into right and obedience into duty.

Father's experiential structure is already complex when he 'disciplines' Junior. We can assume that father has been complexified since youth by his own family and by the society within which he lives. He came to believe that it was bad for boys to feel and express fear; it was a sign of weakness; boys needed to be strong, etc. Not only his family but his entire society reinforced this notion. So in order to live in his situation, father constructed a false self. In ours and many other male-dominated societies, men tend to cover up their fear with aggression. Aggression is supposed to give the appearance of strength. If a man can force someone to do his will, then that is a sign of strength. So father adopts the aggressive false self and it is this self that abuses Junior. Father rationalizes the legitimacy of his behavior by identifying himself with the others in his society that operate out of the same complex structure.

So when father, as an adult, sees Junior sticking his finger in the light socket, he immediately feels fear. But he rejects the legitimacy of that fear and replaces it with aggression. He then acts upon Junior out of a complex structure.

The degree to which we act out of complex structures is the degree to which we are not experiential beings. The degree to which we act out of SSR structures is the degree to which we are experiential beings. It is the moral task of human beings, according to experientialism, to act as experiential beings and to treat each other as experiential beings.

- ### *Levels of Consistency*

Consistency refers to the relation between components of experience within one experiential structure, between a given set of experiential structures, and between people who participate in their own experiential structures. In consistent experiential structures, components of the structure are SSR. There is an absence of complexity. The extent to which an experiential structure is SSR is the extent to which it is consistent; conversely, the extent to which an experiential structure is complex is the extent to which the structure is inconsistent.

When the components of one experiential structure are consistent, then the structure is consistent on the intra-experiential level (i.e. one experiential frame or structure). When a set of structures are consistent with each other in regard to the issue, topic, or subject expressed in the cognitive component of the structures and all individual structures are SSR, then consistency is achieved on the inter-experiential level. These experience can occur adjunctively (serially) or disjunctively (at different times).

For instance, if a person sincerely believes that the earth is flat, acts as if it is flat, teaches others that it is flat, etc., and the structure of the experiences within which he participates is SSR, then consistency exists on intra- and inter-experiential levels. Such experiential structures are referred to as beliefs.

Beliefs can either be learned and accepted as one's own or imposed from without, i.e. by another person or persons. In our previous example, Junior learned that touching light sockets was off limits to him. He learned that such an act could hurt him badly. He accepts on trust that this is so, or he could learn this directly by actually experiencing a shock. Such learning is SSR, i.e. intra- and inter-experientially consistent.

But when Junior is physically and emotionally abused by father, he 'learns' to stay away from the light socket but at the expense of denying an integral part of his identity, i.e. the SSR structure that informed him that his curiosity and behavior were right and good, i.e. his real self. This type of learning is complex; it is an ontological distortion and a moral bad. It is inconsistent on the intra- and inter-experiential levels of consistency.

When the person who believes that the earth is flat begins to participate in experiences that conflict with his flat-earth experience, e.g. why does the bow of the incoming ship point up at a distance and is flat upon approach to the dock? or why didn't I get from point X to point Y at the time calculated according to my (flat-plane) geometry?, then the experiential structures in regard to this issue are in conflict. Structurally, they are both SSR, but topically, they contradict each other. This set of experiences, as discussed before, is referred to as compound. Much learning occurs within the dynamics of compound structures.

In our other example, Junior participates in a compound structure when his mother sets limits on his behavior. His curious experience conflicts with his off-limits experience until he comes to accept the legitimacy of his off-limits experience and acts in accord with his newly acquired belief that lights sockets are off limits to him if he doesn't want to get hurt.

Likewise, the flat earth experience comes into conflict with the round earth experience until the round earth experience prompt enough confirmation experiences so as to replace the flat earth experience with the round earth experience. One belief is replaced by another belief.

Using another historical example, we know that Darwin's rejection of creationism and his positing of evolution to explain the origin of the species did not occur overnight and without internal struggle. But once the evolution experience replaced the creation experience in Darwin's experiential structure (acceptance), and the evolution experiences were strong enough to support his revealing this belief to others (assertive confrontation), then Darwin was in position to grapple with the responses of others and either to reject or affirm his experience. If Darwin did not have the strength to affirm his experience (belief) in the face of criticism, rejection, and attempts at oppression, then someone else would probably have been credited with the theory, and Darwin would have suffered the same fate as Junior's submission to his father. He would have denied his own experience and submitted this part of his identity to the values of others.

At the point in history when Darwin conceived the idea that we evolved over time rather than being created in an instant, let's say that he was alone in this belief (even though he was not). Over time he gained confirmation experiences that strengthened his growing belief. This was who Darwin was, i.e. an evolutionist. Eventually, he told someone else and gained confirmation experiences on the interpersonal level of consistency when the other person agreed with him. Now we have consistency on the mutual level, a belief sincerely shared by two people. The belief spreads to a group of people and we achieve consistency on the group level. But there is a vast array of groups in the world, some that very well might not agree with Darwin and to which Darwin might have actually belonged. So Darwin might have experienced consistency in relation to members of one group (i.e. his group of evolutionists) and conflict in relation to other groups (e.g. church, family, etc.)

Darwin's spreading of his theory can be understood as an assertive confrontation but only inasmuch as he owned his own objective claim. Unfortunately, it seems that history is bearing out that Darwin's claim is of the traditional objective variety where one objective claim (creationism) is replaced by another objective claim (evolution), even though the new objective claim is methodologically less absolute and unchangeable. But for the sake of illustration, we will imagine that Darwin's claim (theory) was owned and, hence, the experiential structure within which he participated was SSR.

A consistently structured belief originates either from the individual person's connection to herself and her environment or from another person who shares their own experience with that person. Darwin shared his belief with others, and others sincerely accepted or agreed with him until the society, in general, within which he lived accepted or agreed with his belief. Once the general society accepts the belief, we have achieved consistency on the societal level of experience, depending upon the structure of the society.

If a given society (or nation) is politically structured as a democracy, then consistency can better proliferate. People will come to accept a belief on their own accord, according to their own lights. If the society is hierarchically structured (e.g. monarchy, oligarchy, totalitarianism, aristocracy, etc.), then beliefs tend to be formed from the top by the few or the one elite and imposed upon all the others.

Hierarchies admit of, encourage, and promote dominant: submissive relationships. Monarchies and totalitarian regimes allow one individual to have unilateral power over all others in the society, oligarchies and aristocracies several individuals. Businesses, even in democratic societies, are overwhelmingly structured hierarchically.

When Darwin spread his belief of evolution, he spread it primarily within a hierarchically structured society. Though England was politically a democracy with a nominal monarchy at the time Darwin promulgated his theory, business was primarily hierarchically structured. Also, that society was primarily Christian, which is strongly hierarchical in regard to Catholicism and weakly hierarchical (more democratic) in regard to some sects of Protestantism.

If the theory of evolution were experiential in nature, it would spread as beliefs might spread through a democracy, where other individuals are free to judge for themselves whether or not the belief is sound. But since evolution tended toward being a traditional objective belief, it landed up rivaling the current objective belief that dominated the society at the time, i.e. Christianity, and therefore hierarchical structures continued to dominate social systems.

In order for consistency of experience to be reached on all levels of experience, no one will be able to dominate another person. No one will be able to impose his or her will upon another without the other freely allowing him or her to do so.

In our example above, Junior freely allows mother to impose her will upon him because he trusts that her will, in this case, was better than his own in promoting his well-being. But Junior did not freely allow father to impose his will upon him. He 'allowed' it but only because his identity was altered so that he could survive in that relationship. To freely allow someone to impose his or her will upon one entails that that allowance is a part of a series of consistent (SSR) experiential structures. The formation of complex structures is indicative of altered identities that serve to form dominant:submissive relationships. Dominant:submissive relationships form the basis of hierarchies. Therefore, ideas that spread within hierarchies tend to align with established traditionally objective ideologies or are constitutive of new traditionally objective ideologies.

Transforming hierarchies into democracies creates organizations that are conducive to assertively confronting complex structures. False selves are confronted while real selves are affirmed and complexified individuals are transformed into experiential beings. As experiential beings, people tend to know themselves better, be themselves, and deal effectively with the consequences of being themselves. They tend to repel people's attempts to impose their will upon them, and they tend not to impose their will upon others. As such, their vote in democratic elections reflects their own values rather than the values of others.

The last level of consistency is the inter-societal level, where societies or nations interact with other nations. If Darwin's theory of evolution could be seen as a way to democratize knowledge of human origins over and against the relatively rigid absolutism of religion and the hierarchical organizations it promotes, then evolution could be understood as a theory at least tending toward democracy. Since the sciences are populated by more people than the clergy, and since access to the physical world of the sciences is a relatively equal opportunity access, then the sciences can be seen as more democratic in the construction of knowledge. But, unfortunately, as argued above, science in general tends strongly toward the traditional objective assumptions of realism, and, hence, whatever gains have been made by the democratization of knowledge have been mitigated or negated by the 'objectivizing power' of realism, serving only to replace one traditional objective hierarchical system (religion) with another (science), the former with a supernatural component, the latter without.

In addition to this, the theory of evolution has expanded into explaining human behavior as well as human origins. In doing so, evolution maintains that hierarchies are natural, biological human systems of organization, and that men, when together in groups, will naturally tend to form hierarchies. Since there have been no genes found to support this claim to date, sociobiologists have had to use as evidence the overwhelming number of political hierarchies in the world and, if they decided to exploit another area of existing hierarchies, the overwhelming number of hierarchies in business organizations. They point toward the differences in biology between men and women to account not only for the great number of existing hierarchies but also for the fact that men, rather than women, tend to dominate hierarchies. Combine such an ideology with the fact of global male domination of organizations and we have ideological 'justification' for male-dominated hierarchies.

Contradicting this theory is the fact that democracies are increasing around the world, and that even sociobiologists tend to decry the 'fact' of male domination and hierarchies in general as biologically determined. Sociobiologists tend to accept hierarchies as natural, but they don't like them. They are hard-put in trying to explain why democracies are tending to proliferate around the world today. Democratic tendencies seem to be going against nature.

When evolution, like theistic theories, is seen through the eyes of experientialism, the ideas that constitute the respective ideologies become relativized, and the experiential structures within which the adherents to these ideologies participate become objective. When this occurs, we can scrutinize the experiential structures of those promoting these ideologies. When the theory of evolution is applied to social behavior, it aligns well with religious ideologies that uphold the superiority of men over women and the two generally opposing ideologies join forces to help perpetuate male-dominated hierarchies throughout the world. The experiential structures that constitute the perpetuation of such ideologies are wracked with complexity.

Let's use one example among many to support this point. Some Arab countries are supportive of clitorectomies, i.e. the removal of young females' clitorises. These countries are non-democratic and ruled by men. How might such a practice become acceptable to people? If we analyze, at least hypothetically, the experiential structures of the people who might support such a practice, we might find complex experiential structures.

It has already been argued that men tend to be socialized to deny their own fears and replace their fears with aggression (e.g. the Junior example above). A similar analysis might apply here. If men fear women leaving them and fear the idea that they can't hold onto their woman and might lose them to another man, then developing ways to make sure that their woman stays faithful to them by controlling them makes a certain rational sense. Men want to achieve X (faithful woman), so they create rule Z (mandatory clitorectomies). If they can utilize the Rousseauean idea and change force into right and obedience into duty, then they can get women to believe that men have the right to create and enforce such a rule and that women have the duty to comply with it. Now we have a complex structure that has been socialized into a meta-experiential construct. It forms part of an ideology that is passed down from generation to generation.

Men and women are people and people are naturally experiential beings (refer to Junior example and core self analysis above). When their being experiential beings is rejected or negated through abuse, complex structures are formed, and the false selves that are created through the complexification of experience will tend to collect together with similarly complexified individuals, to express themselves through traditional objective ideologies, and to form dominant:submissive relationships on the social level (i.e. hierarchies).

Consistency of experience on all levels (intra-experiential, inter-experiential, and interpersonal: mutual, group, societal, and inter-societal) is the overarching aim of experientialism. Individual as experiential beings assertively confront other individuals, especially those operating out of complex structures, in order to maintain experiential consistency; groups can do the same to groups; societies can do the same to societies. But such a task is difficult and will take considerable effort and time to accomplish.

5. Reason, Free Will and Determinism

William James pitted rationalism against empiricism and listed traits for each (James, 1981):

The Tender Minded (Rationalism)	The Tough Minded (Realism)
Rationalistic (going by 'principles')	Empiricist (going by 'facts')
Intellectualistic	Sensationalistic
Idealistic	Materialistic
Optimistic	Pessimistic
Religious	Irreligious
Free-willist	Fatalistic
Monistic	Pluralistic
Dogmatic	Skeptical

This division represents types of persons more than differing ontological stances. Understood experientially, the rationalists refer to those people who are inclined toward primatizing or consistently focalizing the cognitive and affective components of consciousness, whereas the empiricists refer to those people who are inclined toward primatizing or consistently focalizing the behavioral, sensual, and environmental components of experience. The rationalist feels comfortable in dealing with thinking and feeling in relation to self (relativistic leaning), whereas the empiricist feels comfortable in dealing with sensing and behaving in relation to the physical world (objective reality). The rationalist looks inward; the empiricist looks outward. Historically, the rationalist, though inherently to some degree relativistic, has tended to be objectivistic. The supernatural rationalists (reified rationalists) offer God as the ultimate reality, whereas the natural rationalists (Descartes, Kant, Hegel, et al) offer mind and spirit as ultimate reality. Historically, the empiricist, though inherently to some degree relativistic, has tended to be objectivistic. The materialists (reductive empiricists) offer matter as the ultimate reality, whereas the quantum physicists contend that energy is the ultimate reality, and it is not exclusively made of matter but a combination of matter and non-matter.

On the issue of explaining human behavior, the free willists line up with the rationalists, and the determinists (James's fatalists) line up with the empiricists. The free willists conceive of human behavior as a mental triadic process: desire – free will – behavior, whereas the determinists conceive of it as a physical triadic process: environmental stimulus – organism – response. For the free willists, there exists a metaphysical space between desire and behavior in which we choose what we do. For the determinists, the process is completely physical and the triadic division is merely a conceptual way of explaining the process. The problem with both conceptions, from the experientialist point of view, is that they are linear and, hence, reductive and over-simplified. They are both missing the big picture.

In regard to the free willist camp, desire is not an independent phenomenon that can be separated from other components of experience in order to account for human behavior. We must cognize some sort of thought in relation to any affect, and the thought is that which "gives us direction" or "points us toward" someone or something so that we might act in that direction. A thought gives us a possible course of action. But any possible course of action is necessarily connected to a particular behavior. We cannot think without already acting in some manner. Simply because a thought might concern a future behavior does not mean that no behavior is engaged in at the time the thought is conceived.

One idea that James did not include in his divergent lists was "reason". I think that this quality is not on either list because it is used by both parties. The free willists, whether of the supernatural or the natural ilk, understand reason to be a faculty or capacity of mind that we humans employ in order to decide between two (or more) possible courses of action. For most rationalist-oriented people, free will is a metaphysical reality that somehow acts or causes physical reality to move. For the determinists, reason is used illegitimately as a faculty of mind that somehow guides materialistic causal thinking. The materialist position on reason has been so self-contradictory and muddled that it is no wonder rationalist-oriented individuals criticize it so much. If reality is ultimately comprised of matter, and behavior can be explained by how some types of matter cause other types of matter to move (behave), then it seems to follow that reason cannot tell us that this is so or guide us in this activity, because reason is only matter in motion just like everything else. Logic, which is used extensively by scientists and philosophers of science, is nothing more than certain processes of matter in motion and, hence, is part of the cause/effect chain. How can something that is a part of the materialist process be used to guide our thinking about that process? In order for materialism to be consistent with itself, reason must be a type of matter in motion, probably brain matter in motion. Once it is so conceived, then materialism will align itself with experientialism.

In order to elucidate the problems with the rational and empirical slants on why human behavior occurs, I will analyze an example of human behavior and the processes that precede it experientially. John and Lana are in a room talking to each other. John desires to kiss Lana. The experiential structure within which John participates might look like this:

Focal Consciousness		Peripheral Consciousness
Cognition:	kiss her	oriented, familiar with things in room, etc.
Affect:	lust	comfortable in environment
Behavior:	looking at her lips	breathing harder, slight sexual excitation, etc.
Sensation:	her lips	hearing her speak, smelling her perfume, etc.
Environ:	her	in room
"I":	ownership	
SSR		

Let's say that this experience is simple, strong and right (SSR). If it is followed by the behavior of kissing her, the experience may change to:

Focal Consciousness		Peripheral Consciousness
Cognition:	kissing her	oriented, familiar with

		things in room
Affect:	satisfaction	comfortable in environment
Behavior	kissing her	touching her body, heart-rate increasing, etc.
Sensation:	her lips	her body, his heart beating, increase sexual stimulation, etc.
Environ:	her lips	her body, in room
"I":	ownership	

In neither of these experiences does there appear to be anything called reason. There doesn't appear to be any alternative courses of action being considered. There is only one course of action and that is to kiss her. There isn't any significant doubt about whether or not this action is morally right, whether or not she will reject his kiss, or whether or not he really wants to kiss her. There is only one course of action that enters his mind, and that is to kiss her. If all human actions were to take place like this, then the idea of reason would not exist. We'd simply have an idea which would be supported by a feeling, a behavior, a set of sensations, and an environment, and unless something occurred to alter this course of action, then the act would occur. There would be no reflection upon it, no hesitation, and no conflict.

If there is no conflict in experience, then there is no reasoning. There is simply movement in the direction that experience dictates. Only when a conflict in experience arises can we talk about reasoning.

Let's revise our lust-experience to look like this:

	Focal Consciousness	Peripheral Consciousness
Cognition:	kiss her	oriented, familiar with things in room, *knows he's married*
Affect:	lust	comfortable in environ
Behavior:	looking at her lips	breathing harder, slight sexual excitation, etc.
Sensation:	her lips	hearing her speak, smelling her perfume, etc.
Environ:	her	objects in room
"I":	ownership	

His next experience might look like this:

Cognition:	I shouldn't do this; I'm married	*her lips*, oriented, familiar with the things in room
Affect:	duty	*uncomfortable in environ* slight guilt over thought of kissing her
Behavior:	looking away from her	hearing the sounds in the room, breathing slows, sexual excitation decreases, etc.
Sensation:	the floor	hearing sounds, objects in room, *pain in stomach*
Environ:	the room	objects in room
"I":	ownership	

Let's say that the duty experience is the same strength as the lust experience. We'll assign a number to its strength on a 0-10 scale, 0 representing very weak and 10 representing very strong. The number for the first experience when it obtains is 5. John's desire to kiss Lana is stronger than his interest in talking to her. Had nothing happened to alter this course of action, he might very well have kissed her. But within John's peripheral consciousness is the knowledge that he is married. He wasn't focused on this thought when he thought of kissing her, but it was there. It might very well have been focalized a number of times throughout his interaction with her prior to this point, but it wasn't accompanied by a set of components strong enough to prompt a change in the course of his behavior. Had the thought of his being married prior to this point been focalized in consciousness, it might have looked like this:

Cognition:	watch it, you're married	her cleavage, knows where he's at, knows what she is saying, wonders if she knows what he's thinking
Affect:	caution	becoming slightly uncomfortable with situation
Behavior:	looking at her face	blinking 'innocently' (covering)
Sensation:	her face	sounds of her talking, objects in room
Environ:	his being in the room with Lana	objects in room, etc.

"I": ownership

The caution experience is immediately replaced by this experience:

Cognition:	understanding what she's saying	knows where he's at, believes his brief lusting has gone undetected, etc.
Affect:	interest	lust, becoming more comfortable
Behavior:	looking at her face	nodding, shifting in chair
Environ:	Lana in room	objects in room, etc.
"I":	ownership	

If we say that this caution experience is weighted as a 2, then it might very well be followed by a continuation of a comfortable conversation between a man and a woman. Gazing at Lana's cleavage was not enough to prompt an experience that would redirect his course of action, so he continues his conversation. But when he looks at her lips, the experience is followed by the kiss-her experience, which is weighted as a 5. This immediately prompts a duty experience, which, let's say, is weighted as a 5. Now John is in conflict. His conflicting experiences prior to this point (i.e. his cleavage experiences) were not strong enough to put him in serious conflict with himself, but this kiss her-experience is.

Now John will participate in a series of experiences that we will call reasoning. His kiss-her (lust) experience is followed by a conflicting duty experience, each possessing equal strength. He cannot suddenly remove himself from the flow of experience and pick one course of action over the other; this is impossible. He cannot remove himself from experience, 'look at' the two courses of action, pick one that suits him, and increase its strength so he could act accordingly. Rather, he must participate in a series of experiential structures that will, at some point (we'll say) render only one course of action. The experiential process that leads to that one course of action is called reasoning. The experience that ends the process of reasoning and establishes one course of action is referred to as a decision.

In all of this there is no evidence of any faculty of reason. Rather, there are conflicting experiences that admit of conflicting courses of action (different cognitions) which work themselves out, with John as an inextricable part of the process. Experientially, reason is not a faculty of mind but a series of experiences that are in conflict with each other. No conflict, no reasoning. No reasoning, no faculty of reason to account for it. Reason, as a faculty of mind, is a meta-experiential construct, i.e. an idea or concept that refers to a supposed ontological reality (faculty) that somehow influences or controls experience itself. But when reason is subject to experiential analysis, the faculty of reason becomes redundant and distorting of reality. To posit that we have this faculty of reason is to buy into the distortion that this faculty can actually be manipulated or used to produce rational thought and behavior.

Now let's return to our original example:

Focal Consciousness		Peripheral Consciousness
Cognition:	kiss her	oriented, familiar with things in room, etc.
Affect:	lust	comfortable in environ
Behavior:	looking at her lips	breathing harder, slight sexual excitation, etc.
Sensation:	her lips	hearing her speak, smelling her perfume, etc.
Environ:	room	room
"I":	ownership	
SSR		

which is replaced by:

Cognition:	kissing her	oriented, familiar with things in room
Affect:	satisfaction	comfortable in environ
Behavior	kissing her	touching her body, heart-rate increasing, etc.
Sensation:	her lips	her body, his heart beating, increase sexual stimulation, etc.
Environ:	her lips	her body, in room
"I":	ownership	

In this set of experiences we cannot find anything that resembles free will. And if what I have contended up to this point is true, i.e. that we cannot remove ourselves from experience, then there is nothing 'between' or 'above' these two experiences that might 'house' free will. There is no transcendent ego or self that makes it possible for one experience to shift into the next experience. In this set of experiences there aren't any conflicting courses of action (cognitions). There's only one thing to do, i.e. kiss her, and there's only one thing being done, i.e. kissing her. If there is only one course of action in experience, then there is no free will.

Traditional free will requires that there exist at least two possible courses of action: do X or not do X. Christian ethics holds that we can either act in accordance with our desire or not. Regardless of the desire, we will always have the possibility of not doing X. But in our example, if X is "kiss her," then what is 'not X'? John does not entertain the notion of not kissing her at this moment; he only thinks of kissing her. And there is nothing in the experience that supports the idea that John should not or cannot kiss her. The "not" supposedly resides in the metaphysical space between desire and action that traditional theories of free will maintain exists. But if desire (affect) and behavior are co-existent, as experientialism maintains, then there is no metaphysical space between the two. Neither is there any metaphysical space between experiential structures. Neither is there any metaphysical space surrounding the set of experiential structures where we might find optional courses of action. In this set of experiences, there is only one course of action. If there is only one course of action, then there is no decision being made. And if there is no decision being made, then by definition, there is no free will in use.

When conflict is introduced and reasoning takes place, then the conflicting experiential structures within which the person participates *will work themselves out* according to their own structures, in conjunction with the person. For instance, in the set of experiences below,

Focal Consciousness		Peripheral Consciousness
Cognition:	kiss her	oriented, familiar with things in room, *I'm married*
Affect:	lust	comfortable in environ, *guilt*
Behavior:	looking at her lips	breathing harder, slight sexual excitation, *hesitation*, etc.
Sensation:	her lips	hearing her speak, smelling her perfume,

slight twinge in stomach

Environ:	her in room	objects in room, outside of room, etc.
"I":	ownership	

which is replaced by:

Cognition:	too far; I'm married	kiss her, oriented, familiar with things in room, etc.
Affect:	guilt	comfortable in room but uncomfortable in situation
Behavior:	glances away	slight shot of adrenaline, nervous eye blinks, decreased sexual arousal
Sensation:	adrenaline rush	hearing her speak, objects in room, hearing her speak, smelling her perfume, etc.
Environ:	room	objects in room, outside of room, etc.
"I":	ownership	

which shifts quickly to:

Cognition:	I shouldn't do this; I'm married	image of her lips, oriented, familiar with the things in room
Affect:	duty	lust, comfortable in environ but uncomfortable in situation, slight guilt over thought of kissing her
Behavior:	looking away from her face	looking at lips, hearing the sounds in the room, breathing slows, sexual excitation decreases, etc.
Sensation:	the floor	hearing sounds, objects in room, pain in stomach
Environ:	the room	objects in room
"I":	ownership	

though John is thinking "kiss her", he is peripherally aware of his being married. If he did not possess any sexual loyalty to his wife, he may very well have not even been aware that he was married; or if he was so aware, it would probably be for different reasons (e.g. getting caught). So there exists conflict within experience.

The understanding "I'm married" is supported by the affect of guilt, the behavior of hesitation, the sensation of slight twinge in his stomach, and her as slightly shifted out of focus in the room. This combination of components constitutes a peripheral experience that possesses its own structural independence. And this peripheral structure is strong enough to prompt the next experience where John recognizes that he's gone too far. The fact that he's married breaks into focal consciousness and is accompanied by increased guilt, a hesitation that has shifted into glancing away, an adrenaline rush, and Lana shifting into the periphery of consciousness.

In the focal kiss-her experience, the "I" is peripheral; John is focused on Lana's lips. The conflicting peripheral structure is strong enough to prompt its shift into focal consciousness. John does not have the power to choose for this to happen. He cannot suddenly remove himself from the flow of experience, consider the focal kiss-her experience and the peripheral I'm married-experience, strengthen the I'm-married experience, insert himself back into experience and feel a full-blown guilt. This is impossible. He cannot control the weight or strength of the peripheral and focal structures. *He* is not somehow detached from experience (e.g. transcendent ego) and capable of manipulating experience as he sees fit. Rather, he is an integral part of experience. He is an inextricable part of the experiential flow.

One problem with the traditional notion of free will is that it allots more power to the person than is the case. Once experience can be analyzed into its components, we can see that free will as a faculty or power evaporates. But this does not mean that determinism is in position to 'win the day'. Even if all of these experiential components are correlated with biological events in the body (which I suspect they are), the materialistic triad of environment – organism – response is too simplistic to capture the dynamic interdependence of the mind-matter synthesis (components of experience).

Part 3: Experientialism and Materialism

1) Materialism and Determinism

Materialistic determinism assumes that the environment is not only separate from the mind but that the mind is a product of, and wholly dependent upon, the environment. Environment (matter) is all there really is, so if we are to understand our behavior, we need to understand the causal links between the environment and our bodies. Historically, science has gone about this task in a simple linear fashion. But with the advent and development of neuroscience, science is realizing that this linear causal method is too simple, that the brain is divided into integrated, overlapping areas that reflect the components of experience that have been delineated in this work (e.g. cognitive, affective, motor (behavior), and sensory areas). But the reductive tendencies are still very strong. These tendencies are reflected in the development of the philosophy of science that assumes that the world is ultimately made of matter and that the environment is ontologically separate from the body (which contains the 'mind').

But as I've already argued, if the environment were removed from consciousness, then all objects outside of us - all space, and our own body, inasmuch as we could be aware of it - would be gone. If consciousness were still to exist, how would we characterize it? What would we be conscious of? Our own thoughts? If we were conscious of our own thoughts, then how would we characterize them? Since there is nothing outside of our own thoughts, except perhaps, 'us', then what would we be thinking? Memories of past objects of sensation? But these wouldn't exist because there would have been nothing for us to have sensed. Imaginary objects? Images of what?

Bickle argues that the direct stimulation of the brain using electrodes to produce "personal experiences" sidesteps sensory input and virtually eliminates the environment as a causal factor of phenomenological data (Bickle, 2003). This argument makes sense only within the confines of the framework of reductive materialism. If one targets matter as ontological, then scrutinizing material things in this fashion is quite reasonable. The neuroscientist virtually disregards the experiential structure within which he (let's say) participates and concentrates his attention, literally, on the matter before him. Penfield and Newsome focused on brains, electrodes, monitors, and behavior of subjects; they concerned themselves with themselves only inasmuch as they described their behavior and their thinking in regard to the matter before them. Such descriptions were "used" to get to the reality of matter.

If experience is understood as componential, then the environmental component within which Penfield participated consisted focally of brains, electrodes, monitors, and behavior in front of him and peripherally of objects in the laboratory within which he worked - the walls and windows of the lab, all sights, sounds and smells in the room and outside of the room that impinged upon his senses - and his own body. This accounting would include the entire environment within which Penfield operated that was reachable through sensation. Experientially, if Penfield were to understand his own research, he would not only have had to understand the entire environment within which he operated, but he would have had to recognize that that environment was integral to his research. That is, he could not isolate an aspect of the environment (e.g. brains, electrodes and monitors) and expect this to be a sufficient rendering of his research environment.

The same holds true for the people with whom he interacted. For instance, a subject who agrees to have electrodes implanted in her (let's say) brain for research purposes and is conscious throughout the experiment participates in a set of experiential structures that include many but not all the contents constituting the researcher's environmental component of experience (i.e. objects in room, walls, the researcher's body, and her own body). The two will possess different contents within their respective experiences also (i.e. the subject might not see the electrodes being implanted in her brain, etc.)

So when Bickle implies that sensory input is sidestepped and environmental objects are eliminated as relevant factors in the research (or bypassed), he is referring only to those factors that constitute the focus of attention of the researcher. The researcher "flips the switch" (let's say) and sends an electrical current into a part of the subject's brain and then he watches what the subject does or records what the subject says. Since there is no object in the environment to produce what the person experiences, Bickle assumes that the environment has been eliminated in the causal accounting of the behavior of the subject. But this seems to be far from the case. Without the environment, there would not be anyone doing of any research upon anyone else. To eliminate the environment from any causal accounting of anyone's (or anything's) behavior would be tantamount to eliminating reality.

Simply because an electrical current passes through a part of the organism's brain does not mean that the cause of the organism's behavior is simply the electrical current. The current would not have stimulated that area of the brain had not the neuroscientist administered it. We cannot remove the cause of the current from the environment when accounting for the behavior (or "personal experience" of the subject); the cause, in good part, is the neuroscientist. After all, a similar current (not an identical current) could stimulate the organism's brain which was caused by an appropriate object or event in the environment. Simply because the object in the environment is the neuroscientist and the electricity is administered through an electrode does not mean that the cause of the organism's behavior has suddenly disappeared from the environment. All the neuroscientist does is replace one environmental cause (normally occurring object or event) with another (himself). Experientially, the electrical current is primarily instrumental, and only secondarily "causal". [1] It is *that which is used* by the scientist to produce a behavioral response. It is causal only within the framework of the materialist, who tends to abstract himself from his own work.

Reductive materialists are leaning toward the cellular biology of the brain to found ultimate material components. They are altering genetic material so as to determine what genetic basis there is for cognitive and emotive phenomena. For example, a neuroscientist might clone a mouse and tamper with its DNA, thus producing a mouse that does not possess long-term potentiation (LTP), which normal mice possess (Bickle, 2006). When the tampered mouse shows behavioral evidence of impaired long-term potentiation, the neuroscientist concludes that that area of the DNA is responsible for long-term potentiation.

If we analyze the experiential structures within which the neuroscientist is participating, we might find something like this:

Cognition:	I'm altering the mouse's DNA at point X
Affect:	intense interest
Behavior:	using technique to alter DNA
Sensation:	mouse's DNA
Environ:	laboratory
"I":	ownership

which is eventually 'joined' by:

Cognition:	mouse doesn't show signs of long-term memory
Affect:	excitement
Sensation:	mouse behaving in a way that negates its possessing long-term memory
Environ:	mouse in lab
"I":	ownership

---

[1] I use quotes around the term "cause" because, experientially, an object or event in the environment is not understood to be a stimulus that causes electricity in the brain, as it is understood in linear descriptions, but rather as an integral part of a whole experiential structure; it cannot be detached from experience. Hence, our understanding of "causation" will be re-framed (transformed) within experientialist theory, a subject that cannot be dealt with here. Suffice it to say that our linear understanding of "cause" will be transformed into a systems understanding of "prompt," where specific neural networks (e.g. cognitive) will interact with other networks (e.g. affective) within an interactive, interdependent whole system of networks.

which is replaced by:

Cognition: long-term memory can be affected by gene manipulation!
Affect: elation
Sensation: objects in lab
Behavior: extending arms in air (or however this researcher would behave)
Environ: lab
"I": ownership

In none of these experiences does the researcher transcend or remove himself from the structure of experience to prove his contention. "Long-term memory can be affected by gene manipulation" is ontologically a thought or an idea and not a reality-beyond-experience or a condition-of-experience. The neuroscientist cannot get beyond experience to make good his claim. He can only alter experiential contents. No matter how many times he conducts the experiment, he does not get beyond the structure of experience. He only *believes* or *thinks* (assumes) that he does. But such a belief must be false, and such knowledge must be a distortion of reality. For if we cannot get beyond experience to determine 'reality', then experience *is* reality. And to posit conditions that make experience itself possible, without realizing that the positing of those conditions is actually components of experience, is to create a meta-experiential construct, i.e. to distort reality.

Bickle argues that "behavioral data is fully explained by the dynamics of interactions at the lowest level at which we can intervene directly at any given time to generate behavioral outcomes, along with the known anatomical connectivities throughout neural circuits leading ultimately to effects on muscle tissue attached to skeletal frames" (Bickle, 2006). Simply put, tampered mice exhibit behavioral evidence of long-term memory loss; monkeys exhibit arm raising after an electrical impulse is discharged into their brain, etc. Let's assume an experientialist position and agree with the neuroscientist. "Electricity administered to the brain causes behavior in an organism." As a cognitive component of experience, this conclusion is perfectly valid. But when the scientist abstracts himself from the environment within which that conclusion is conceived, then he distorts reality.

2. Materialism Made Experiential

If we analyze the experiential structures within which the researcher participates, we will see something like this:

Focal Consciousness	Peripheral Consciousness
Cognition: 'flipping switch at time T'	belief that apparatus is working properly and that electrical current is passing into monkey's brain; objects in room, etc.
Affect: confidence	possibly a little excitement or fear (which alters belief slightly
Behavior: 'flipping switch'	sitting, hunching back, blinking eyelids, heart beating, etc.
Sensation: 'switch'	objects in room, sounds and smells, pressure against finger, etc.
Environ: 'switch' in room	objects in room, sounds and smells, etc.
"I": ownership	

which later changes to:

Cognition: monkey is raising arm at time T1	belief that raising arm is caused by electrical current objects in video tape, objects in viewing room, etc.
Affect: excitation	possibly a little vindication (which would alter the cognition a bit)
Behavior: viewing the video tape	smiling, body taught, heart beating faster, etc.
Sensation: monkey in video tape	monkey in video tape's surroundings, objects in viewing room, etc.
Environ: video tape in viewing room	objects in viewing room, etc.
"I": ownership	

When we analyze the experiences, we *do not find* any electricity at all in the environmental component of experience. We *do find* it as an idea in the cognitive component of each experience. This shows that the researcher has not gotten outside of the experiences within which he participates. Rather, at most, he 'believes' or 'assumes' or 'is certain" that electricity-beyond-his-experience caused the monkey to raise its arm without recognizing (owning) that that knowledge lies within the cognitive component of experience. He, in effect, disowns his own experience by asserting the objectivity of the electricity and its causal properties in relation to the monkey over and above his own experience.

I'll argue that any attempts he makes to transcend the experiential structures within which he participates will land him back in experience. When he "thinks" he is outside of experience and doesn't own his own thought, then he is creating a meta-experiential construct, i.e. a "dis-owned" objective reality.

From the experientialist perspective, objective reality is integral to experience, where experience is defined as a necessary combination of cognition, affect, behavior, sensation, environment, and the "I" (ownership). We hold electrical currents (and anything else we sense in our environment) as real-beyond-experience because we experience them to be so. But experiencing them to be so (i.e. experiencing them to be objective) does not mean that they are so (objective-beyond-experience). We cannot *get* beyond experience to determine this 'fact'. The best we can do is experience it to be so. Whether there actually is an electrical current out there beyond our experience of it being there is inconsequential. To use a pun: it doesn't matter. What matters is that we assume, are certain, or believe that it does exist out there.

The problem that the experientialist has with the materialist is not that the materialist assumes, is certain of, or believes that the electrical current (or anything else) is actually objective and independent of his own personal experience (this everybody does); the problem is when he doesn't own his own objective experience, when he doesn't realize that the objectivity lies *in experience* as a whole and not in the environment. Experientially, the environment cannot be abstracted from experience, and still have experience. The environment of the materialist is an experiential construction, and when it is not recognized as such, it is a meta-experiential construct, or a distortion of reality.

So when the determinist claims that brain activity causes muscular activity in the body, we must recognize that the claim is a content of the cognitive component of experience and not the 'capturing of an environmental reality' through intellectual and linguistic means. Once this is admitted, then determinism is transformed into relationships between experiential structures.

Also, beyond the realm of determinism and firmly planted in the realm of ontology, the materialistic neuroscientist who claims that thoughts are equal to neuron activity in the brain is necessarily in error unless she (let's say) owns her own claim because she cannot remove herself from the experiences within which she participates. For instance, let's say that someone has invented goggles whereby one can directly see the neurotransmitters being transmitted by neurons in one's brain. This experience would look like this:

Cognition: those are my thoughts!
Affect: excitement
Behavior: looking at neurotransmissions
Sensation: neurotransmissions
Environ: neurotransmissions in brain
"I":   ownership

In this experience there is nothing that we can call thought except the word in the cognitive component of the experience. The neuroscientist is sensing neurotransmissions in her brain, not thoughts. She *believes* that those neurotransmissions are her own thoughts. The fact is, she cannot remove herself from the experiential structure within which she participates in order to determine that what she is seeing is actually her own thoughts.

Therefore, what the materialistic scientist does is to illegitimately remove herself from the experiential structures within which she participates, splits ontology into two aspects (internal (mind) and external (matter)), forgets or denies the internal aspect, and then reduces the internal aspect to the external aspect. All of this is experientially acceptable. But unfortunately, more often than not, the materialistic scientist goes one step further: she believes she has captured reality-beyond-experience by disowning her own claim. In other words, she creates a meta-experiential construct or distorts reality.

References

Augustine, St. *On Free Choice of the Will.* Macmillan Publishing Company. New York, NY. 1964.

Aquinas, Thomas. *The Pocket Aquinas.* Pocket Books. New York, NY. 1960.

Berkeley, George. *Three Dialogues Between Hylas and Philonous.* Prometheus Books. Buffalo, NY. 1988.

Bickle, John. *Philosophy and Neuroscience: A Ruthlessly Reductive Account.* Kluwer Academic Publishers. Dordrecht, The Netherlands. 2003.

Bickle, John. "Reducing mind to molecular pathways: explicating the reductionism implicit in current cellular and molecular neuroscience." Synthese. Springer Science + Business Media. B.V. 2006.

Bruner, J.S. Early social interaction and language acquisition. In H.R. Schaffer (Ed.), *Studies in mother-infant interaction.* Academy Press. London. 1977.

Descartes, Rene. *Discourse on Method and The Meditations.* Prometheus Books. Amherst, NY. 1989.

Ekman, P. Universals and cultural differences in facial expressions of emotion. In J.K. Cole (Ed.). *Nebrasksa symposium on motivation, Vol 19.* University of Nebraska Press. Lincoln. 1971.

Foucault, Michel. *The Archaeology of Knowledge.* Pantheon Books. New York, NY. 1972.

Hegel, G.F.W. *Phenomenology of Spirit.* Oxford University Press. Oxford, England. 1977.

Heidegger, Martin. *Being and Time.* State University of New York Press. 1996.

Hume, David. *An Enquiry Concerning Human Understanding.* Prometheus Press. Buffalo, NY. 1988.

Hume, David. *A Treatise of Human Nature.* Penguin Books. New York, NY. 1969.

Husserl, Edmund. *Ideas.* The Macmillan Company. New York, NY. 1931.

James, William. *Pragmatism.* Hackett Publishing Company. Indianapolis, Indiana. 1981.

Kant, Immanuel. *Critique of Pure Reason.* P.F. Collier. New York,

NY. 1902.

Locke, John. *An Essay Concerning Human Understanding. Dover Publications.* New York, NY. 1959.

Marx, Karl. *Economic and Philosophic Manuscripts of 1844.* Prometheus Books. Amherst, NY. 1988.

Piaget, J. *The Origins of Intelligence in Children.* Basic Books. New York. NY. 1954.

Plato. *The Republic.* Prometheus Books. Buffalo, NY. 1986.

Plato. *Theaetetus.* Hackett Publishing Company. Indianapolis, Indiana. 1992.

Rousseau, Jean-Jacques. *On the Social Contract.* Hackett Publishing Company. Indianapolis, Indiana. 1987.

Russell, Bertrand. *The Problems of Philosophy.* Prometheus Books. Buffalo, NY. 1988.

Sartre, Jean-Paul. *Transcendence of the Ego.* Noonday Press. New York, NY. 1957.

Stern, Daniel M. The Interpersonal World of the Infant. Basic Books. Perseus Books Group. 1985.

Warner, Heinz. *The Comparative Psychology of Mental Development.* International University Press. New York, NY. 1948.

INDEX

ALSO BY G. MICHAEL BLAHNIK

Novels

Denial: A Tale of Love, Sex and Modern-Day Madness
The Queen of Spades

Plays

What God Has Joined
The Investment
The 20th Quarter-Annual Horse Contest
Solitary God
A Woman of Means
Dead Cowboys
No Tomorrow
Joe Dick, P.I.: The Perfect Crime
Head and Hands
Sex in the Library

Philosophy

Experience: An Exploration into the Structure and Dynamics of Human
Consciousness
Sense, Sex and Sin: Foundations for an Experientialist Ethics
Experientialist Ethics: A Comparative Study

Psychology

Emotional Investment: Transforming Psychotherapeutic Assumptions

Made in the USA
Coppell, TX
07 July 2021

58672265R00083